SAY YES TO
Spirit

A Personal Journey for Developing SPIRITUALITY RECOVERY and HEALING

LEO BOOTH

Health Communications, Inc.
Deerfield Beach, Florida

www.hcibooks.com

Library of Congress Cataloging-in-Publication Data

Booth, Leo, 1946–
Say yes to your spirit / Leo Booth.
p. cm.
ISBN-13: 978-0-7573-0729-4 (trade paper)
ISBN-10: 0-7573-0729-9 (trade paper)
1. Spirituality—Meditations. 2. Devotional calendars. I. Title.
BL624.2.B66 2008
204'.32—dc22

200704840

Publisher: Health Communications, Inc.
3201 S.W. 15th Street
Deerfield Beach, FL 33442-8190

Cover photo ©PhotoDisc
Cover design by Larissa Hise Henoch
Interior design and formatting by Lawna Patterson Oldfield

Foreword: Treating Heroes

I met Rev. Leo Booth at an addiction conference in Sea Island, Georgia. I remember he was discussing the difference between spirituality and religion, and he was one of the first speakers to openly discuss religious abuse: how one can be hurt and shamed in the name of God.

The message immediately resonated with me because as a young man growing up in Albany, New York, I had often been made to feel like "a bad boy" by my religion. I feared God had given up on me and so . . . why try? And although I saw myself at times as a "tough guy," I secretly feared my Roman Catholic God. We had priests and nuns who were truly kind and whom I respected, but there were clergy who seemed to enjoy humiliation and corporal punishment. I knew my upbringing (including my religious upbringing) was dysfunctional. Rev. Leo gave me a context in which to see and understand my religious abuse, and I was grateful.

When Rev. Leo spoke about spirituality, however, he lit up the room—telling jokes, standing on chairs. Referring to John Lennon and Oscar Wilde, he made spirituality come alive and easy to understand. Reverend Leo's definition was simple and yet profound; spirituality is about being a positive and creative human being. That's it!

Jesus was positive and creative. Mother Teresa was positive and creative. Dr. Martin Luther King Jr. was positive and creative, and, yes, I also am positive and creative.

After his talk, I met with Rev. Leo and asked him to speak to the patients and staff with whom I work at Behavioral Health of the Palm Beaches in South Florida. He came, he spoke, and I hired him to be our spiritual director.

From the earliest days of my recovery from alcoholism I had intuitively known that spirituality, a love of God beyond the words of religion, was essential. I also knew recovery involved a love of self and the people around me. At some level I had grasped that although I struggled with my many imperfections, God had *accepted* me, and I wanted to take this message to my family, friends, and patients at Behavioral Health of the Palm Beaches. From the beginning the treatment facility had always encompassed spirituality, but I wanted it to be *more* spiritual. Meeting Rev. Leo Booth had given me the opportunity to live my dream.

Rev. Leo Booth is not only a colleague, he is also a friend. I admire his enthusiasm, his inclusiveness, his vulnerability, and his willingness to grow. In this book, *Say Yes to Your Spirit,* he not only writes for the alcoholic and addict but also for the family, the significant others, and the friends who have been touched by this disease. Indeed, anyone reading this book will benefit from its powerful messages:

- You have the spiritual power to change your life.
- God wants to partner with you in creating your success.
- In this dance in God you have certain steps to take.

Through the course of my life I have become an avid reader and have become enamored with the myths of the world. The ones that have affected me the most were those of the hero's journey. In them I saw the story of recovery. Myths tell the story of overcoming the demons and dragons that stand in the way of the prize. In this uplifting, comforting, and useful book, Rev. Leo provides the tools and inspiration for you and your loved ones, so that you may begin your own journey toward becoming a hero, with the prize being the dance we do in God in recovery.

—Donald K. Mullaney, Ph.D., LCSW
Certified Addictions Professional

Acknowledgments

When writing a book you come to value the friends and colleagues that you have around you. This book, *Say Yes to Your Spirit,* was the creation of many valuable minds, many comments I've heard along the way, too many discussions over coffee until late into the night. Always there are some people who stand out.

Kien Lam supported the initial concept and added ideas while he typed the script. He's been my office manager for many years and is my most cherished mentor.

Hilary Fitzsimmons and Michael Schultheis, who work in my office, read and reread the early scripts, again presenting improvements that have enhanced the book.

Michele Matrisciani, who as editorial director at Health Communications worked tirelessly to improve the writing and tighten up my thoughts, helped make *Say Yes to Your Spirit* vivid and clear.

Gary Seidler, who planted the seed, is a trusted friend. I know that more will be developed from having his professional vision.

Dr. Don Mullaney kindly wrote the Foreword for this book and allowed me to develop new spiritual concepts with the patients at his facility.

And lastly, I thank Peter Vegso, publisher at Health Communications, who said yes immediately to the initial concept of this book and made it happen.

Have I left people out? Yes. Forgive me, but you are not forgotten in my feelings of gratitude.

Introduction

Some years ago, I was privileged to write a daily meditation book for alcoholics and addicts called *Say Yes to Life*. Published by Health Communications, the book became popular with the recovering community and treatment centers.

Family members came to me and asked if I would be writing a similar book for "everyone"; people who do not necessarily have an addiction but want to read a positive spiritual message each day. Thanks to this suggestion, I now present to you *Say Yes to Your Spirit*. Now I realize that when I say I'm writing this book for "everyone" this is extremely general. However, truth to tell, throughout this book I'm really focused on *recovery* issues. And it has been my experience that the vast majority of people are recovering from something! I'm trusting that these people will benefit from reading *Say Yes to Your Spirit*.

Since writing the original book I like to think that I have grown; indeed my understanding of our relationship with God and Spirituality has moved in the direction of our *taking responsibility for the life we wish to live.* Metaphysical people call this philosophy cocreation.

What does that mean? Well, in a nutshell it suggests that God's Spirit is alive in each and every one of us and our responsibility is to reflect it; manifest the divine. But more than this, cocreation is being actively involved in creating a better, safer, and more accepting world. God not only created us but is divinely involved in his creation; creating us to create.

The template I have used to reflect this philosophy is *Dancing in God.* When I was originally thinking about this book I had thought the grammatically correct phrase *Dancing with God* as a description, but it really didn't go far enough. Today I believe that God is not only with me but *in* me, and me *in* him. Dancing with God implies *separation* whereas (poetically speaking) Dancing in God reflects my belief that wherever I am God is . . . and all is well. I am not separate from Divine Energy and this makes me powerful in my dance toward recovery, health, prosperity, and healing.

A constant theme that I heard from my mother, when I was growing up, was "God helps those who help themselves." The seeds of cocreation were being *sown.*

This meditation book challenges us, on a daily basis, to step up to the plate and create a better life, a better world.

I trust you are ready to *Dance in God.*

—*Rev. Leo Booth*

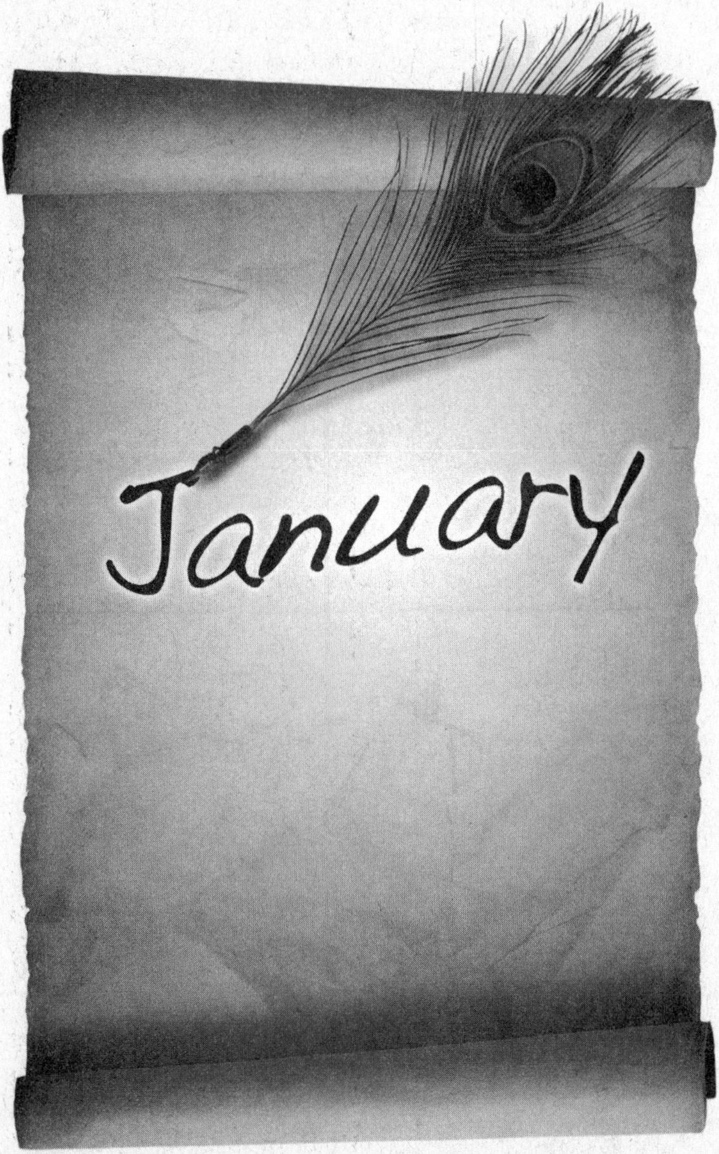
January

Dance

Today I am dancing in God.

—Leo Booth

When I first thought about a title for this book I wrote "Dancing with God." It seemed a more correct statement—more respectful, more objective. People dance *with*. . . .

But this statement did not capture what I wanted to say. Today I believe that we are dancing *in* God.

Metaphysical writers affirm that God is not only outside of us but within. We carry the presence of God, and we can choose partnership with Spirit to reflect this truth.

Spirituality involves the combination of God and creation. I believe this. There is no separation, only appearances.

In my dance in God,
I am reminded that there are steps
that only I can make.

Religion

One religion is as true as another.

—Robert Burton

Whatever *Say Yes to Your Spirit* is, it must be more than denominationalism. I am a Christian because I was born into a Christian family who had me baptized before I was six months old in Manchester, England. Incidentally, that is probably why I always overcook my vegetables!

We are born into a culture, born into the color of our skin, born into our race, and also born into our religion. Few people, in the scheme of things, change their religion.

Spirituality is understanding respect, not just a respect for the culture of other people but also their beliefs. And as I implied above, most religious beliefs are taught to us as children.

This awareness helps me to dance in God and with the foreigner on a daily basis.

My respect for you includes
your religious beliefs.

Work

Work is the curse of the drinking classes.
—Oscar Wilde

Oscar Wilde was a very funny man. He usually created humor within a statement that had a kernel of truth. It's hard to work if you are drunk!

Say Yes to Your Spirit is a choice. It embraces a spirituality that involves not just saying prayers but also taking care of your body. It is practical.

Alcoholism is rampant in our society. But even if you are not an alcoholic, you can drink too much. Today we embrace the concept of responsibility. Our energy is depleted if we overdo anything.

How can we dance in Spirit if we are tired, drunk, or high? We all need to embrace a healthy lifestyle so that we can appreciate God's world.

Today I seek to do nothing that will harm my body.

Survival

Life gives challenges; challenges often bring strength; and strength will enable us to survive.
—Kien Lam

It is not unusual to hear people saying, "There is no gain without pain." All of us will face some challenges in our lives. Alcoholism and drug addiction are some of the pain that we discover in life. Other people have different aspects of pain.

Being a survivor is one way of saying that we have faced a problem and overcome it. The spiritual concept of "courage" is involved, and we should be proud of our achievement. All of this is involved in the *Say Yes to Your Spirit* philosophy.

Life will certainly bring challenges. They can be faced, and we can be victorious. This is good to know.

Today I am willing to face my challenges so that tomorrow I can dance in God.

Creativity

The best way to predict the future is to create it.

—Author Unknown

For most of my childhood I received the religious message that if God wanted you to have something then he (God was always a "he" in those days) would make sure that you got it. Also, it followed, if you didn't get something or have something in your life, it was because God didn't want you to have it.

If you wanted something very much, then it helped to pray in church, light a candle, or put some money in the collection box. Priests suggested that God is pleased by a healthy donation!

I didn't hear very much about creating what we wanted or needed in our own lives. The idea of "pray hard, but remember to move your feet!" was absent from my Sunday school. When I eventually heard the co-creation message (the concept of partnering *with* God to create what you want) at Unity of Christianity, it made so much sense; incidentally, it also made me successful.

I am involved in my life and success.

Problems

Problems cannot be solved at the same level of awareness that created them.
—Albert Einstein

I'm not sure exactly what Albert Einstein is saying, but I do know that problems can be solved. We must, however, be willing to face them.

Say Yes to Your Spirit is about reality. And things do go wrong. In most cases, if we are willing to face the actual situation, they can usually be put right, or at least we can mitigate the damage. However, occasionally we can do nothing except accept the damage, and that is the solution.

Problems can sometimes help us rise to a higher solution. To accept the problem of alcoholism enables potential recovery. Acceptance of a failed marriage can lead to freedom and happier alternatives.

Our dance in God presupposes challenges.

Today I examine my response to problems.

Lies

How can you love a liar? They are not present.

—Maud Booth, my mother

If you are a liar, you create a story about your life that is not real. Liars are not present. They make things up. For this reason they cannot be trusted.

We all tell lies at times. Some are told to be kind:

- "I really like your hat."
- "What interesting furniture."
- "Your little boy is very active!"

Some lies—in England, we call them "fibs"—seem part of the social contract. But lies that take you away from reality, lies that mislead, are very dangerous. They also stop you from being loved, because you are absent in the fantasy you have created.

Most times, better to tell the truth.

Today I know that honesty
is the best policy.

Reality

If you want the rainbow, you must put up with the rain.
—Unknown

A popular saying in recovery circles is "No pain, no gain." Everyone, including me, seems to understand this, yet it verges on being a mystery: why is so much growth and achievement accompanied by pain?

I don't know. And I don't really need to know. If I was to hazard a guess it might be because *change* is involved.

- To enjoy recovery from alcoholism we need to change our drinking habits.
- Serenity might require we walk away from an abusive work environment.
- Discovering a God as we understand God might necessitate leaving the church of our childhood.

Change usually follows something that is not working, and when a thing is not working it can be frustrating and painful.

Say Yes to Your Spirit *to discover the rainbow.*

Hope

The hopeful man sees success where others see failure, sunshine where others see shadows and storm.

—O. S. Marden

I have a few good friends who are optimists. They always see the good in people. They don't dwell on the painful or negative. They enjoy the moment. Yes, they are people of hope.

And because of this *Say Yes to Your Spirit* attitude, they are happy. They look healthy. Always ready to laugh. Always ready to dance.

Hope is an attitude. It can be developed in our lives. It is a style. Also, it is contagious. You catch it from people. Negative people create negativity. Hopeful people create hope.

Look and see who are the people in your life.

My belief in creativity
forever brings hope.

Neighbor

In the field of world policy I would dedicate this nation to the policy of the good neighbor.
—Franklin Delano Roosevelt

There are some things that we intuitively know to be right . . . good . . . spiritual. Probably the most famous story that Jesus told was the parable of the Good Samaritan. That story resonates with how people should really live, how people should treat the afflicted. God asks us to demonstrate the love that keeps the world at peace.

Who is my neighbor? Some people think it is only the person next door or our fellow citizens. But when we embrace the concept of *Say Yes to Your Spirit* we realize that our neighbor is our fellow human being, regardless of race, culture, or creed. Only then will the world be at peace.

Today I am a citizen of the world.

Perfection

He that is without sin among you, let him cast the first stone.
—Jesus

I'm reminded of a story that is told in recovery circles that says that each time you point a finger at another person, there are three fingers pointing at yourself.

Usually I criticize in people what I most dislike in myself. And I've discovered that when you really get to know a person, really understand them, they are usually lovable. When I visit a prison to give a lecture I always leave feeling that "there but for the grace of God, go I."

None of us are perfect. And yet, metaphysically, when we understand this, we grow closer to perfection. I've always felt that it is my failings that build a bridge to others, not my achievements.

Say Yes to Your Spirit helps us keep this awareness and remain humble.

In the awareness of my failings,
I am made whole.

Nobility

When a man has pity on all living creatures, then only is he noble.
—Gautama Buddha

I saw a man on the freeway putting himself at risk to save a runaway dog.

Occasionally, I see a lady in my local park feeding the ducks.

When I'm at the airport I occasionally observe a blind person being helped by a guide dog.

Love, concern, and trust are all aspects of *Say Yes to Your Spirit*. And none of this is complicated. The above stories that include animals are all everyday experiences. None of them are complicated theory. Rather they represent feelings. They are an emotional response to life.

Nobility is demonstrating love as a response to the many happenings in our life. It is the love dance.

Today I am able to appreciate the creatures who share our planet.

Freedom

Freedom is the right of every human being.

—Rev. Martin Luther King Jr.

Spirituality is a choice. Recovery is a choice. Living the life that says *Say Yes to Your Spirit* is a choice. All the above happens because we make it happen—the power of being human—and it brings freedom.

This freedom is also a choice. The poets, who write during times of persecution, tell us that you can throw people in prison, torture them, chain them, separate them from loved ones, but you cannot take away the freedom that lives in their souls.

Having this attitude is a choice. It is a choice to believe in the all-encompassing entity called spirituality. It is a choice to dance in God.

Today I choose freedom.

Reality

Lead me from the unreal to the real!
Lead me from the darkness to light!
Lead me from death to immortality.
—The Upanishads (Hindu scriptures)

I love the above quotation. It reminds me of so many of the Christian hymns I used to sing as a child, beginning, as they did, with the refrain, "Lead me."

Today in the philosophy of *Say Yes to Your Spirit* I also realize that I need to be willing to lead myself. It is not always going to be clear that God is "leading me." I'm not always going to hear the call or feel the pull. Today I need to intuitively know when it's time to move. This is cocreation.

God is all around. And God is also in me. I'm not only waiting to hear the still small voice. I'm also ready to say the words.

Today I'm ready to get up
and do my dance.

Humility

Humility doesn't allow people to walk all over me.

—James Baldwin

The word "humility" has often been misunderstood. James Baldwin understood this.

Christian piety often gave the impression that it was spiritual to let others take advantage of us—and we suffered in silence.

But *real* humility involves respect. It is necessary to respect other people, treating them with dignity and genuine interest. But we must also respect ourselves.

Say Yes to Your Spirit affirms this balance. I'm not respecting you if I allow you to disrespect me.

I affirm a humility that respects self.

Enemies

The Bible tells us to love our neighbor and also to love our enemies, probably because they are generally the same people.
—G. K. Chesterton

Recently I've caught myself saying that the reason I find it hard to love a person is because I don't know them . . . really *know* them . . . understanding the wounds and warts that make up their lives.

This is true with my enemies. The people we don't like are usually the people that we don't understand. Once I try to really understand my enemies I cease to hate them, or dislike them, with any intensity.

This awareness is the key to *Say Yes to Your Spirit*. My enemy is really my neighbor in strange clothes.

Today I can love my enemies.
And often they become my friends.

Belonging

I knew that if I cut a tree, my arm would bleed.

—Alice Walker

Sometimes I hear myself saying that I never met a stranger. What I mean is that once I overcome my fear to talk with you or engage in some way, it's usually a pleasant experience.

I'm often in the company of people whom I don't know very well. But once I share my story, my joys, my fears, my hopes, my confusions, I usually find that we can have a conversation. And then a connection is made, especially if I'm willing to listen to their story.

Underneath the pomp and circumstance we are all very much the same—all trying to make sense of this thing called life.

When I am known,
I belong.

Law

Useless laws weaken the necessary laws.

—Charles de Montesquieu

Sometimes we say that we fear the law. But laws are helpful, as long as we allow them to breathe, grow, or change.

I can't remember who said it, but the saying is that all laws are made to be broken. That saying makes us think.

If we look at the history of the laws that supported religious persecution, segregation, and sexism, we realize that most laws can be manipulated to serve our own selfish needs.

Say Yes to Your Spirit is seeking to live the Golden Rule: treat other people the way you would like to be treated.

Now *that* is a necessary law.

Spiritual laws are spiritual tools to help us love. And with the love comes the dance.

Prejudice

Prejudice is never the answer.

—Gandhi

Jerry Jampolsky says that there are really only two emotions: love and fear.

Prejudice is really about fear. It can be wrapped up in sophisticated language, but it is really about fear. We fear what we do not know.

Love is about recognition and connection. Only when I'm able to overcome my own fears am I able to love you . . . and conquer my prejudices.

Say Yes to Your Spirit helps me overcome my fears.

I know that love is in
my own interest.

Christianity

Christianity is not the same as churchianity.

—Anonymous

I've always loved Jesus. From being a little boy I knew that he was a good man, helping people, teaching people, sometimes chastising them. But his bottom line seemed to be that love makes more sense than hate.

The history of the church, indeed the history of most organized religions, has often included judgment, wars, persecution, and hate. Now, I know this is not the whole story. There have been great men and women in all religions who have stood for truth, but they were usually martyred—killed by the faithful!

Say Yes to Your Spirit affirms an inclusive spirituality that is based on respect. It is the dance of Jesus.

I am ready to dance in Spirit.

Popularity

What's right isn't always popular, and what's popular isn't always right.
—Quintin Hogg

I caught myself recently laughing at a joke that was not funny; it was also disrespectful to a minority group. Why did I laugh? Because the group I was with was laughing.

I've done this before. And I don't like that part of me that is a people-pleaser.

I've been seeking to *Say Yes to Your Spirit* for many years, and I've been attracted to men and women who were prepared to stand alone: Golda Meir, T. E. Lawrence, Gandhi, Margaret Thatcher . . . and of course, Jesus.

I recognize that our dance in God will sometimes require that we separate ourselves from the crowd. We may appear to dance alone. At times I have done this, and I'm quietly proud of myself.

What about you?

I understand that doing the right thing for me isn't always popular with others.

Goals

It is important to have goals in life. What may not be achieved today can always be achieved tomorrow.

—Kien Lam

Say Yes to Your Spirit is always about having a positive and creative attitude in life. And goals point the way to achievements.

This book is a case in point. Some years ago I'd written *Say Yes to Life*, a daily meditation volume for addicts. And then I began to think about family members and friends who were not addicts, but who would benefit from a positive message each day. I had a goal to write this book.

If you are reading this book, then you will see that my goal was achieved. And it didn't happen overnight! For nearly a year I set aside some time to write something for each month . . . and the rest is history.

When I am dancing in God I am still able to focus on my goals.

Brevity

Never say more than is necessary.

—Richard B. Sheridan

God is love. Spirituality is the demonstration of that love. And we all have it.

Say Yes to Your Spirit is affirming this knowledge in every moment of our day. If we fail, we start again. It is the *effort* that creates greatness.

I've said enough.

Less is more.

Self

Whenever two people meet, there are really six people present. There is each man as he sees himself, each man as the other person sees him, and each man as he really is.

—William James

I understand that *Say Yes to Your Spirit* is a journey. It is a journey into self.

For years I was lost. I had all the trappings of success: job, friends, house, family, religion, but inside I was lost.

Then I slowly began to realize that the purpose of life was the discovery of self. Where does my fear come from? What do I need to make me happy? What are my goals in life? Only when I was prepared to look within myself, could I be at peace with God, the Universe, and others.

This journey is ongoing, beyond death. And it is fun.

Hello, self!
I'm coming to find you.

Ambition

The child without ambition is like a watch with a broken spring.

—R. W. Stockman

There is a positive aspect to ambition. It is about success, prosperity . . . getting what you think or do *out there* for others to see. It is about wanting to make this world a better place. It involves pride. Ambition is a good thing.

Arrogance is something different. These two words that begin with "A"—arrogance and ambition—get confused in the minds of many people.

Say Yes to Your Spirit is ambitious. It wants to influence the world to a creative One-ness. It respects all cultures and religions but affirms a spiritual connection. *Say Yes to Your Spirit* believes that wars and divisions will end when people experience that common humanity and need for each other. And it's attainable.

I am spiritually ambitious.

Nature

Nothing is evil which is according to nature.

—Marcus Aurelius

Oscar Wilde once said that a book is not good or bad; it is either well written or not.

Sometimes we think that something is evil because it is different. Gay people have suffered from prejudice, as have people of color.

Today more people understand that what God created is not evil. Our true nature is never evil. And there is a wonderful tapestry to life.

This is the theme of *Say Yes to Your Spirit*. The things from God are true and real; they are blessed.

I embrace the full implications of my nature.

Dogma

Dogma is less useful than cow dung.

—Mao Tse-tung

Dogma suggests that something is divinely written and it will never change. Incidentally, when the church or religion has pronounced "a dogma," it has usually regretted it.

Dogma is not very popular among spiritual people because it tends to be rigid, judgmental, and arrogant. When we *Say Yes to Your Spirit* we seek to avoid these attitudes and behaviors.

The God I believe in dances with me, and if Chairman Mao were still living, God would also dance with him. Heck, I would dance with Chairman Mao!

I'm dogmatic about not wanting dogma in my life.

Insight

Having eyes do you not see?

—Jesus

When we *Say Yes to Your Spirit* we develop spiritual gifts that not only help us live but help us live with others. One such gift is insight.

We are able to see beyond the outward exterior, beyond the pretense, see through the hypocrisy. How? Because when we embrace Spirit we have the confidence to really look at people, developing the eye of knowledge.

If we want to develop the gift of insight we need to be healthy. We need to heal our physical, mental, and emotional attributes so that we can enthusiastically, intuitively *Say Yes to Your Spirit.*

Today I dance with my eyes open.

Country Music

I love country music. It is in my soul.

—Miles Adcox

Only recently have I been aware of the richness and comprehensiveness of country music. I like it because it usually tells a story . . . a sad story.

It is not unusual to hear about poverty, alcoholism, violence, cheating, divorce, and sexism. But it sounds so good.

It sounds good, the rhythm and poetry, but it can also make you think . . . and cry. *Say Yes to Your Spirit* is about hearing and growing from the many stories of life; country music recounts many of them.

Long live Willie. We miss you, Johnny.

I'm crazy, and I want to dance in God.

Potential

Treat people as if they were what they ought to be, and you help them to become what they are capable of being.
—Johann W. von Goethe

I have come a long way in my life: not just the distance between England and America, but the journey into wisdom, recovery, and personal healing—saying *Say Yes to Your Spirit.*

There have been rough times along the way, deep valleys that needed to be crossed, high mountains that only I could climb. Life is never smooth.

But something else helped me. I had family and friends who allowed me to walk my journey. They nurtured my journey in life by respecting my individuality. And with that came my potential.

I respect people enough to let them live their lives.

Sex

Sexual pleasure, wisely used and not abused, may prove the stimulus and liberator of our finest and most exalted activities.

—Havelock Ellis

S*ay Yes to Your Spirit* involves sex. It is a gift from God—a gift that needs to be valued, respected, and developed.

Religion has often given the message that sex is dirty, wrong, sinful . . . the *thing* that should not be spoken about. The result: shame.

Many people are dying in this shame. Some are healing. It is important to understand the all-encompassing nature of *Say Yes to Your Spirit.* It involves cultivating the best that is in this world. Sex should not be excluded.

A key ingredient of sexual pleasure is respect.

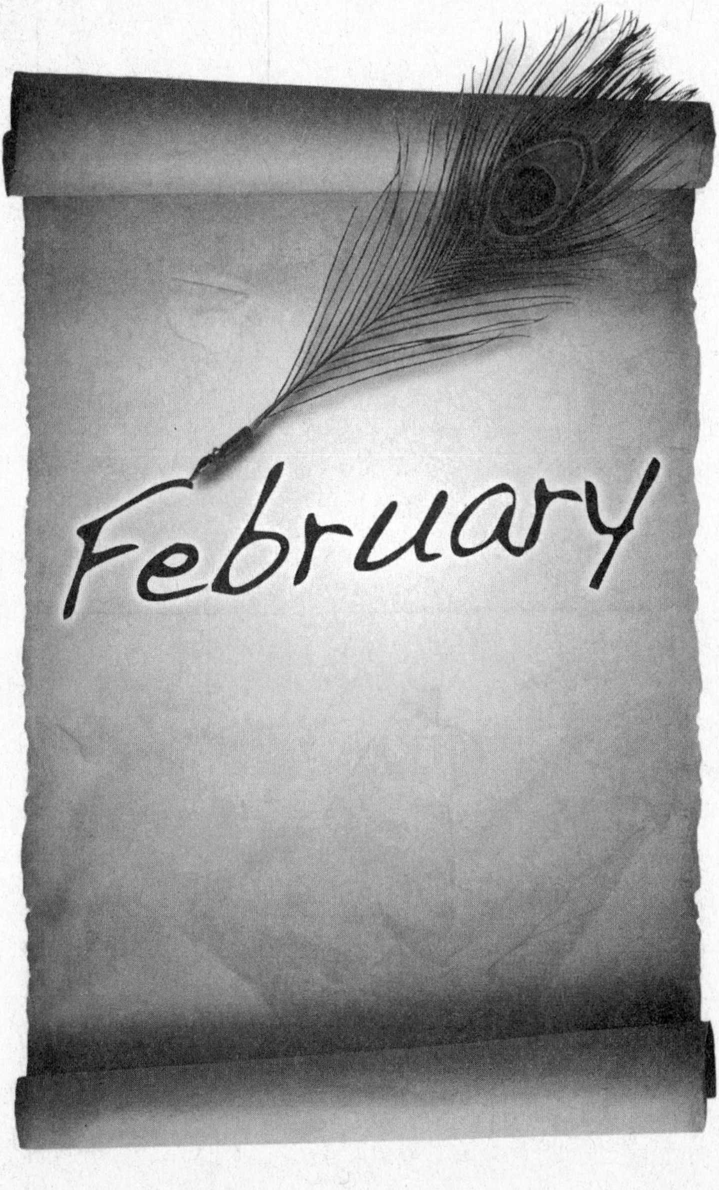
February

Spirituality

There is something of God in each one of us. The challenge is what we are going to do with this divine manifestation.

—Leo Booth

It is so easy to say that God is within each human being. Unity Church of Christianity proclaims that "Wherever we are, God is."

But what does this really mean? I believe that we should step back from the rhetoric and consider the magnitude of this gift . . . and the challenge.

Each day we have a choice, a role to play in the demonstration of God in our lives. We are the eyes of God, so we should seek beauty in the ordinary world around us. We are the voice of God, so we should consider, as Don Miguel Ruiz says in *The Four Agreements*, "the impeccability of our words." We are the feet of God, so we should walk the path of peace and reconciliation.

The divine has become flesh. Let us begin the dance of love.

Today I know and hear God's music in my life. Together we create the dance.

Isolation

No man is an island, entire of itself; every man is a piece of the continent, a part of the main.
—John Donne

I think people love this poem because it speaks of our *connectedness*. Although there are different religions, cultures, races, and colors, we are essentially *one*.

But this poem is describing something far more profound than the connection of the human race. It is our unity with creation, our unity with the energy of the universe, our connectedness with God.

We dance with passion and spontaneity when we know that we belong—that we are not only part of, but reflectors of, creation and the Creator.

Our life is a universal dance.

Today I choose not to give energy
to isolation or separation
in my life.

Freedom

You must do the thing which you think you cannot do.
—Franklin Delano Roosevelt

When I *Say Yes to Your Spirit*, I am saying yes to responsibility. I have the ability to respond to life, all of life: the healthy and the wounded.

Divinity seems strangely broken in many parts of the world. Some people still suffer racism, poverty, religious oppression, and dictatorships. This is real. My spirituality has never been Pollyanna-ish. Some people need not only my prayers but also my help.

Jesus said, "Whatever you did for one of the least of these brothers of mine, you did for me." (Matthew 25:40)

When I fight for freedom, I am freed.

I know I dance with energy when I am free.
This is true for my neighbor.

Change

To exist is to change, to change is to mature, to mature is to go on creating oneself endlessly.
—Henri Bergson

Spirituality is about change. Why? Because spirituality is about life, and life is always changing.

To resist change is to resist life, and this involves God. When we resist change, we are resisting God.

When we understand that God is alive in each of us, then resisting change is self-defeating. Opportunity, growth, prosperity, and peace are all necessarily connected with change; therefore, to resist change is to say no to the dynamic rhythm in life.

God is inviting us to dance in life—to play in life and to take risks. Change is the music to this dance.

I am happy today because I joyously embrace change.

Wonderment

I have had the experience of being gripped by something that is stronger than myself, something that people call "God."

—Carl Jung

Sometimes something happens in life that makes you realize that life is more than personal. It's universal. And the universe contains wonderment.

- I'm flying in an airplane, and I look out at the vastness we call the sky.
- I look up at the mountains with amazement.
- I hear the croaking of a bullfrog on a balmy night in Louisiana.
- A child on the seashore kicks the waves in play.

Jesus said, "Having eyes do you not see? Having ears do you not hear?" (Mark 8:18)

Today I embrace wonderment.

Music

Music happens between the notes.

—Igor Stravinsky

When we *Say Yes to Your Spirit* the world awaits us: with poetry, philosophy, culture, art, and music.

Music is life. We cannot really think it; we can only feel it. Music is to be *felt*.

And our response, usually, is to dance, to join the music. Become one with the music. Express the music.

And even if we don't physically dance, we dance in our mind. Our imagination is fed. Ideas play within the rhythm.

Music is life.

I understand that music happens between the notes.

Health

Good health is the key to happiness.

—Albert Einstein

Say Yes to Your Spirit necessarily involves health. It is not spiritual to destroy my body or my mind or my emotions. Holistic medicine is not an idea. It is a daily practice. So . . .

- I don't eat too much.
- I get rest.
- I see a therapist if I'm stressed.
- I've stopped drinking alcohol.
- I walk every day.
- I express my feelings.

Religion is often a world of prayer, belief, and worship. Spirit opens the door to the universe. Only then can a healthy dance begin.

Health involves choice alongside attitude.

Difference

If Negro freedom is taken away, or that of any minority group, the freedom of all the people is taken away.

—Paul Robeson

We read a few days earlier that "No man is an island, entire of itself; every man is a piece of the continent, a part of the main" (John Donne). And here the thought comes again.

You cannot *Say Yes to Your Spirit* if you say no to life. And life is more than the horizons of my world.

Freedom is not just a word; it's a style in life. It is the opposite of fear and prejudice. It will always find connection in the creative energy of diversity.

Freedom always dances toward the spiritual.

I affirm freedom in the way
I treat the stranger.

Philosophy

Philosophy is not a theory but an activity.

—Ludwig Wittgenstein

Today I understand that the spiritual life is rarely discovered in the black and white, right and wrong, good and bad. That approach to life is too rigid.

When we *Say Yes to Your Spirit* we usually find that spirituality exists in the gray areas of life. We know only a little, but one day. . . .

It is often said in conversation, "I'm not God," meaning the person doesn't know everything. We all need to remember this. The history of human existence is the history of change.

The great spiritual shamans in life instruct us to "dance with doubt" because certainty can be a killer.

Today I understand that I don't know everything. Of this I am certain.

Kindness

Virtue is better than vice, truth is better than falsehood, kindness than brutality. These like love never fail.

—Quintin Hogg

I heard an after-dinner speaker say, "He helped me mostly by his kindness."

I thought about what he had said. I loved my mother because she was always kind to me.

My sister is kind to me.

People get my attention by their kindness. Sometimes we have a tendency to seek for spirituality in the "great" things of life: martyrdom, birth of a nation, great men and women who invent something of wonder, an amazing novel.

But what about being ordinarily kind? *Say Yes to Your Spirit* is how we should live, how we should treat others, how we should treat ourselves.

Kindness is an important value to nurture in our lives.

Today I am learning about kindness.

Acceptance

Sometimes a light breaks into our darkness,
and it is as though a voice were saying:
You are accepted.
—Paul Tillich

In my recovery the value of acceptance has been essential. And it is an aspect of Spirit.

- I can accept a culture that is different from my own.
- I accept that Christians differ in beliefs and styles of worship.
- Today I accept that people can be spiritual without being religious.
- I accept that I am an angel struggling in the dirt.
- I accept the ever-changing dance of life.

It is the differences in life that nurture creativity.

Imperfection

The fault is in us.

—Hannah Arendt

Mahatma Gandhi is supposed to have said that an eye for an eye makes the whole world blind.

My mother said to me once, shortly before she died, that religion scared her because it often seemed so sure of itself. Dogmatic religion is frightening.

That's why I want to *Say Yes to Your Spirit*, because it is gentler. It is less perfect. It accepts the gray in all of us.

We all make mistakes. We say, do, and think things that we wished we hadn't. Oh yes, there is fault in all of us. And that's what makes us so lovable. The Charlie Chaplin tramp is adorable because he is not perfect; he's a wonderful rascal.

I affirm and celebrate the fault in me.

Popularity

Few people are capable of expressing with equanimity opinions which differ from the prejudices of their social environment.
—Albert Einstein

Why do I seek to be popular? I want to be loved. I want you to like me, and this desire to be liked often makes me hypocritical.

In the last few years, as I've danced more and more in Spirit, I find that I'm moving closer to honesty. I still want you to like me, but I need to tell the truth. My truth is who I am. When I betray my truth and seek to appease the majority, I'm uncomfortable.

Spirit is making me more real.
Spirit is feeding integrity into my life.
Spirit makes my life enjoyable.

I want to be popular, but not at the expense of truth.

Love

Let there be spaces in your togetherness.

—Kahlil Gibran

We all need to express love. And when we *Say Yes to Your Spirit* we are affirming this expression in every aspect of our lives.

Love is complicated. It is a small word that says so much. Poets tell us that love can be painful. Life teaches us that it is!

With love we need boundaries. Otherwise we suffocate, and we suffocate the people whom we love. It is at this point that we meet this word called "obsessiveness," the clinging neediness that destroys.

In this book, I've often used the analogy of dance, and dance requires space. Otherwise you trip.

Today I appreciate the spaces in my love for others.

I love with a healthy distance.

Procrastination

Life is wasted in procrastination.

—Epicurus

When I wrote *Say Yes to Life* I realized it was an action book. Spirituality needs to be performed. It is creative.

This is also true with *Say Yes to Your Spirit*. Spirit is breath. It is life. It is energy. And it needs to happen today in our daily life, not talked about for tomorrow.

- Have I called a friend?
- Am I waking up earlier to greet the day?
- Did I go to my recovery meeting?
- Have I begun my exercise plan?
- Did I experience Spirit in my life today?
- Did I tell my daughter I love her?

These are some thoughts that need to be answered . . . today.

Say Yes to Your Spirit *in action.*

Creativity

Why change the world? Change worlds!

—Henry Miller

Spirit is intelligence. It is, for me, the Mind of God at work in and through my daily life. And it often requires reflection.

When I decided to become a Unity of Christianity minister I'd thought about it for many years. It seemed the intelligent thing to do. It is more inclusive than my Episcopal background. It feels right. It is making me into the man I wish to be.

My dance in God has taken me from England to America, into recovery from alcoholism. And now the universe awaits.

Good feeling: an aspect of God's intelligence living in me.

To think is an aspect of Spirit.

Extremists

All evils are equal when they are extreme.

—Pierre Corneille

When I was in China, a tour guide talked to me at length about yin and yang. I didn't understand all that he said, but I grasped the notion of harmony. Spirituality has to be discovered or realized in the balance of life.

That's what extremists miss. They think that excess, louder, winning, even aggression is *more*. Surrender is about understanding that less is more.

Today I know that agreement can embrace difference.

Equality

Treat all men alike. Give them all the same laws. Give them an even chance to live and grow.

—Chief Joseph

My spirituality tells me I am not better than other people. And I'm not less than or inferior to other people either. I'm equal.

Jesus is my mentor. He was a Jewish teacher who seemed to love everybody, if they would let him. Even when he was angry at them I believe he still loved them.

Arrogance, pride, bigotry, prejudice, snobbery: these are the arrows that often slay the spirit. Living with the value of equality is the antidote.

Equality affirms difference; however, it doesn't use difference to discriminate.

Today I treat people the way
I would like to be treated.

Belief

One person with a belief is equal to the force of ninety-nine who have only interest.
—John Stuart Mill

Somebody once asked me, "Leo, what does spirituality or living in the spirit mean to you?"

It means many things. It means making a choice to be positive, developing creativity in my life. It welcomes all the great religions of the world and those that are not so well known. It affirms nature, the universe, and our connection to the animal kingdom.

But it also involves a belief in something that cannot ever be fully explained with words: God, Higher Power, Spirit. It is a *knowing*, a *sense* of being more than any definition.

And it is powerful.

I'm dancing in the power zone.

FEBRUARY 20

Tolerance

I practice tolerance because it is in my interest.
—Voltaire

When we *Say Yes to Your Spirit* we are also saying yes to life, which involves more than just my own life.

I want people to respect my opinions, so I should respect the opinions of others. I want people to consider my religious and political thinking, so I should respect the religious and political thinking of others. Respect and consideration are involved in tolerance.

At the time of this writing the world is very much divided; intolerance seems to be prevalent. Today I tolerate those with whom I do not agree.

I can dance with those
who are different.

Poetry

Poetry helps make life bearable.

—Horace

Spirituality embraces the arts: music, dance, painting, sculpture, and poetry.

Poetry breathes life into a word. Because it uses metaphors and various figures of speech it can say more than a mere description, and we need this when talking about God—when affirming Spirit. Here is an example from the Gospel of Thomas:

The disciples said to Jesus, "Tell us what the Kingdom of Heaven is like."

He replied, "It is like a mustard seed, the smallest of all. However, when it falls into worked ground it sends out a large stem, and it becomes a shelter for the birds of heaven."

Our responsibility is to work the ground.

I prepare the ground for Spirit
to enter my life.

Sleep

As a well-spent day brings happy sleep,
so life well used brings happy death.
—Leonardo da Vinci

What a gift is sleep, to rest. The psalmist said, "Be still and know that I am God."

Part of my *Say Yes to Your Spirit* is rest. I need to sleep and let the busy world go by.

When I was actively alcoholic I seemed to be always rushing around with never enough time. And I missed so much.

Today I go to bed early. Bliss can be a glass of milk and a good book. Then sleep. And in my dreams I get to dance in God.

Sleep is a spiritual gift that
I appreciate today.

Opportunity

Take advantage of the ambiguity in the world. Look at something and think what else it might be.

—Roger von Oech

Years ago I hit upon a definition of spirituality that has worked for me: spirituality is being positive and creative.

I think about this definition almost every day, and it has prepared me for opportunities in my life. I am writing this book after having an early breakfast in Los Angeles with Gary Seidler, an old friend. A part of me didn't want to get up and battle the Los Angeles traffic, but I sensed an opportunity to renew our friendship and it has paid off. He strongly encouraged me to write *Say Yes to Your Spirit*. This is one example of how a friendship has influenced my life.

Life is to be lived, not talked about.

Today I create opportunities in my life.

Honesty

Honesty is the first chapter of the book of wisdom.
—Thomas Jefferson

When I became a minister in Unity of Christianity, I was introduced to the concept of cocreation. Really it is emphasizing a partnership with God. I express this in many ways.

- Placing my hand in the hand of God.
- When dancing in God, remembering that I have certain steps.
- Praying, but also remembering to walk the talk.
- Understanding that miracles involve action.

Honesty also plays a role. I need to get honest. You cannot know me until I practice honesty. There can be no real relationship without honesty. It is the first chapter in the book of wisdom.

I affirm the intention of honesty on a daily basis.

Faith

Nothing in life is more wonderful than faith—
the one great moving force which we can neither
weigh in the balance nor test in the crucible.
—Sir William Osler

I have faith: faith in a creative God, faith in the power of healing, faith in the inherent goodness of all human beings. I'm an optimist.

And my faith teaches me that spirituality and religion are not the same. Usually religion is what we are born into, not unlike our culture. Spirituality is a choice.

That is why we need our own personal definition of spirituality—something that will work for us in our lives. My definition involves being positive and creative because I believe in a positive and creative force in the universe.

That is my faith today.

My faith helps me to be successful.

Wisdom

Education is the key to prosperity.

—Thomas Edison

My mother was a wise woman. Her wisdom continues to live in me. She said, "Anybody who tells you that money isn't important—has it!"

These are wise words. Education helps us to be successful. It helps us to see opportunities, and the result is often prosperity. Wisdom!

It is important to understand that money in itself is not evil. It is really a means to freedom. With it we can travel, help a neighbor, employ people, and generally spread joy.

A wise person understands this.

I aspire to the wisdom that allows me to live abundantly.

Success

Success is what we can make of the mess we have made.
—T. S. Eliot

I understand today that living is part of a continuum . . . and then we die. Many believe that life continues beyond death.

But what do we do with this thing called life? I'm suggesting that we *Say Yes to Your Spirit*:

- Open the door to possibilities.
- Dance in the presence of God, knowing God is dancing in us.
- See the beauty of difference.
- Understand that success and prosperity are attitudes of mind.

It is never too late. Are you ready?

God has given us success.
We need to discover it.

Martyrs

A thing is not necessarily true because a man dies for it.
—Oscar Wilde

When we *Say Yes to Your Spirit* we recognize that we live in a dangerous and violent world. Today I choose not to give energy to the negative and destructive, but to see that the world as it is, wars and all, is part of living in reality.

Crazy exists. People are hurting each other in the name of God. People are creating divisions in the name of God. In the name of God people are being murdered.

What am I going to do? Be careful. Judge the actions and not just the words. Don't rush into anything where angels would fear to tread.

Dance carefully!

Today I affirm reality in my life.

Boredom

The two foes of human happiness are pain and boredom.

—Arthur Schopenhauer

A recent dinner companion of mine asked me, "Leo, am I boring?"

I decided to be honest. "Yes, I'm afraid you are. You've been boring for years."

"Really?"

"Yes, and the reason you are boring is because you are bored: bored in life."

"What should I do?"

"Find the music in life, the spiritual rhythm that makes your existence come alive. And when you find it, dance to it."

Don't think I haven't had that conversation with myself, often. Today I'm dancing.

I'm holding the tail of God's tiger.
And it's exciting.

March

Change

Nothing stays the same. Life is an ongoing dance.

—Leo Booth

I read somewhere that if we keep doing the same thing, then we will keep getting the same results. If we think the same things, then we will keep creating the same outcomes. If we keep saying the same things, then we will keep getting the same response.

Change! And the results are different. It seems so simple. Maybe it is. Perhaps we go into the process of change saying or thinking that it is going to be difficult. But if we realize that change is necessary, and it is in our own interest, then the process becomes more acceptable. What we say we will eventually believe.

I believe that change is necessary for my spiritual growth.

I joyously embrace the concept of change.

Saints

Some people are so heavenly minded that they are no earthly good.
—Oliver Wendell Holmes

I suppose that saints are people who dance in God on a daily basis but don't always know it. Today I want to know it. More importantly I want to live it.

Spirituality involves the physical. Earthly and physical pleasures are divine, and they should be appreciated. For too long we were told that spirituality involved escaping from the body, moving away from the Earth to experience heaven. But heaven is here on Earth. God is to be found in the daily happenings of life. The smile, hug, kind word, and shared meal are all aspects of God.

So many people who say they can't find God are usually looking in the wrong direction. God is here. Everything has the God potential.

God excites me in the dance of life.

Thought

If you want to truly understand something, try to change it.
—Kurt Lewin

This saying makes you ponder. It is a thought that challenges us to think outside of the box. It forces us into explanation.

You cannot really change something without first understanding what it is you want to change. You probably want to change something because you don't agree with it or you think that you have a better solution. And so you really need to understand what it is you want to change.

I am an alcoholic. Only after years of trying to change my behavior and attitude concerning alcohol have I eventually come to an understanding of alcoholism: the denial, manipulation, sarcasm, family history, and mood swings. My efforts at change produced a profound understanding.

I cannot change without thinking.

Inquisitiveness

The person who knows how will always have a job. But the person who knows why will be his boss.

—Carl C. Wood

As a young man I not only wanted to know how a thing works, I wanted to know why. I not only wanted to know what we believe about God, history, and morality, I also wanted to know why we believe it. Sometimes this inquisitiveness got me into trouble, but it has also led to my security in knowing what I believe and why I believe it.

I know that spirituality is different from religion, and I also know why. Spirituality is a more expansive concept. It is more inclusive. It can relate to religion but also refers to the arts. It is poetic: a daily dance in God.

In the "why" questions in life, I take responsibility for my destiny.

God is amazing, and
I am inquisitive.

Nobility

It's easy to make a buck. It's a lot tougher to make a difference.
—Tom Brokaw

I remember saying some years ago, early in my recovery, that I wanted to be noble. It's not a word that is used very often, and yet, can you really be a spiritual person—saying yes to Spirit—without wanting to be noble?

Noble is being honest, humble, patient, kind, accepting, and respectful. It is the strength discovered in a healthy religion. Nobility is involved in our dance in God. It is beyond price.

Money is important. It can bring joy, freedom, and education to many people, but the use of money without the ingredient of nobility is dangerous.

I still want to be noble.

Time

Everywhere is within walking distance if you have the time.
—Steven Wright

When we *Say Yes to Your Spirit* we acknowledge that there is a thing called time; it is the space that makes up our hours, days, weeks, months, and years. We are born into time.

Spirituality teaches us to respect time. Take time. Relax. We can rush at life or we can seek balance. I believe that if we are always in a hurry, rushing, never smelling the roses, then we abuse time. The psalmist suggests, "Be still, and know that I am God." Take a breath. If we are to dance in God, then we need time to make the correct steps, gliding into creativity.

Today we know that compulsion, obsession, addiction, and fanaticism are all unhealthy behaviors because they are frantic. We all need the gift of balance, if we are really to create anything in our lives.

This is the dance.

Today I respect the quality of time.

Soul

The soul that is within me no man can degrade.

—Frederick Douglass

I love words. With words we can create a picture that often leads us to understanding.

I've always believed that the word "soul" appeals to the poet within each of us. If we agree that the soul is not a body part, then what is it?

The soul is that part of us that speaks to our uniqueness, but not just our uniqueness—our divinity. That *something* that understands God, reflects God, is God . . . and breathes through us. And it cannot be taken away or destroyed or degraded.

When we *Say Yes to Your Spirit* we affirm our soul connection to the world and each other. Soul reflects the universal dance.

Wow. I like it!

I nurture my soul with spiritual food.

Character

Character is doing the right thing when no one else is watching.

—J. C. Watts

Spirituality speaks to character. What kind of people are we? What is it that we want to do with our lives? How do we come across to other people?

Hypocrisy is the enemy of true religion. It is most definitely the enemy of spirituality and the molding of a healthy character. Jesus indicated that spirituality involves bringing our lives into the light where things can be seen.

Can we dance in the dark? Yes, but dangerously! It is much better to see where we are going. It is much better for our partners to see where they are going. Spiritual character is attracted to the light.

I am dancing in the light.

Willingness

Nothing is impossible to a willing heart.
—John Heywood

Today I am willing. For many years as a drinking alcoholic, I was not willing. I was not open, enthusiastic, or optimistic. Feeling wounded creates negativity.

In recovery I learned to change, and willingness was an important component of my healing.

- I am willing to change.
- I am willing to take personal responsibility for my life.
- I am willing to accept that diversity is life.
- I am willing to follow direction from the mentors of my choice.

My happiness is related to my willingness to embrace *Say Yes to Your Spirit*. For too many years I danced outside of God. Today I dance in God.

Spirituality includes willingness.

Success

Success has always been easy to measure.
It is the distance between one's origins and
one's final achievement.
—Michael Korda

Success is implied in *Say Yes to Your Spirit.* We can use many words to describe success: healing, recovery, empowerment, prosperity, health. They all imply a choice to improve our lives. Choice is essential. We will get out of our lives what we want. We create our success.

Is God involved? Yes. But God does not make us successful. God does not make us happy. God does not make us prosperous. We are also involved.

This is cocreation. This is the dance in God, and it is the key ingredient that is often not taught in religious worship. We make miracles!

Even in the title for this book, *Say Yes to Your Spirit,* we are the ones saying yes.

Today I understand that
success is my choice.

Perseverance

Few things are impossible to diligence and skill. . . . Great works are performed not by strength, but perseverance.

—Samuel Johnson

"How many books have you written, Leo?"

I tell them.

"That many! Wow. Writing obviously comes easy to you."

Actually it doesn't come easy. I've really got to work at it. I'm writing this meditation at 4 AM—talk about perseverance!

But most things that we achieve take perseverance: marriage, recovery, scholarship, sports, theatre, music . . . the list is endless.

We should also consider that the people who say, "You definitely have a gift," are possibly manipulating the compliment so that they can remain idle. Sloth can be tricky. "If I don't have the gift, how can I be successful?"

Not so fast! We all have gifts. Some of us choose to develop, nurture, and polish them.

We can all learn to dance.

I persevere in my Say Yes to Your Spirit.

Individuality

Whether you think you can or think you can't—you are right.

—Henry Ford

We are all individuals. Some of us are positive and optimistic, believing that we make a difference. Others are negative and pessimistic, believing that we have little value. Which are you?

I realize that there are shades of optimism and pessimism, but attitude is a determining factor in our success or failure. Spirituality is positive. It is always creative and nurtures optimism.

This is the foundation of *Say Yes to Your Spirit*. Because it affirms a positive God, *Say Yes to Your Spirit* creates an energy that always nurtures and inspires. Things will get better.

- People can heal.
- The world is filled with opportunities.
- God is at work within us.
- Whenever we choose we can dance in God.

Our attitude determines our future.

I realize my dance in God starts with me.

Self-Esteem

You teach people how to treat you.

—Dr. Phil McGraw

What an interesting statement. It certainly makes you think.

Why are people interrupting you? Discounting you? Letting you down on a regular basis? Using you? Why?

Maybe, just maybe, you have a role in how other people treat you. Ask yourself the following questions:

- Do you find it difficult to establish boundaries?
- Can you voice and express your concerns?
- Do you set expectations without consequences?
- Do you love others at the expense of self?
- Do you enable abuse by accepting it?
- Are you your child's friend or parent?
- Are you able to "let go" and walk away?

You play a role in the dance you create with other people.

I am teaching people to treat me with respect.

Humor

Before you judge a person, walk five miles in their shoes. That way, when you do judge them, you are five miles away and you have their shoes.

—Freida Norris

I think I received my sense of humor from my mother. She could always find something to laugh about, even in the most serious situations. When I told her I was an alcoholic and needed to stop drinking, she said I would have more money to buy exquisite cheese!

Humor is important. It is an aspect of humility because it stops us from taking ourselves too seriously. We all have problems to face in life, but they usually pass. If we are to dance in God, then we need to be free—and humor helps us to hang loose.

A professor of theology at my university in England said that God created the world for fun. Are you enjoying your life?

Today I'm able to find humor in most of my experiences.

Expand

The only limits to our realization of tomorrow will be our doubts of today.
—Franklin Delano Roosevelt

When we *Say Yes to Your Spirit* we are entering into a more expansive world; the walls of religion, country, and culture are knocked down.

I understand today that my doubts feed my fears:

- I doubt that I will be accepted in foreign countries.
- I doubt that I can learn to speak another language.
- I doubt that God will forgive me.

And I stay afraid.

It is hard to dance in God if I stay in fear. Spiritually I need to confront my doubts that have fed fear into me over the years. The healing begins when I remember, on a daily basis, that God's love is experienced through me, and that with God as my cocreator I can face anything that life throws at me.

I am a winner—period!

The world is my sandbox to play in.

Education

Reading is to the mind what exercise is to the body.
—Richard Steele

Reading allows me to enter into a world that I will never experience personally. I may never go to Iraq, sit in on a meeting with the president, or experience the life and times of Shakespeare, but through reading I am able to experience in my mind all the above and more. Reading helps me to see the future and understand the past.

Dancing in God is timeless. Today I understand that my connection to the universe is nourished through education. I can know more than I can ever see or touch by the power of the word.

On the matter of Jesus's birth, the apostle John wrote, "The Word became flesh and made his dwelling among us." (John 1:14) God's creation comes alive through education, and I am gratified.

Spiritually I am at peace when I sit before a log fire, book in hand, with a nice glass of milk and a chocolate.

I love and appreciate the gift of literature.

Leadership

The very essence of leadership is that you have a vision. You cannot blow an uncertain trumpet.
—Theodore Hesburgh

I suppose it is a truism to say that leaders must lead. But what kind of leader are you going to be?

This is primarily a spiritual book. It seeks to explore what has often been called the Golden Rule: treat people the way you want to be treated. The vision of Hitler or Stalin or Pol Pot has no place in these writings—but the ability to create, shape, and explain a vision is important.

This vision needs to be anchored in a certainty that breeds enthusiasm in those who are following: "This is do-able."

Not only Gandhi, Churchill, and Roosevelt, but also you and me are called to lead in certain circumstances—and conviction is necessary.

I lead with the force of Spirit.

Appreciation

The worst mistake a boss can make is not to say, "Well done."

—John Ashcroft

Recently I caught myself saying in a lecture that religion often tells you what you are not, spirituality tells you who you are. And I liked what I said!

For too many years, as a child, I got the message of original sin: I was imperfect, fallen, a mistake. I was not what I was intended to be.

Today I disagree with this teaching. I am not a mistake. My dance in God is a celebration of this awareness.

I believe that I am a child of God. More, I believe that I am an adult in God, who reflects divine love. This profound spiritual understanding gives me an appreciation of other people, cultures, and religions.

I was not born sinful, broken, or imperfect. Rather I was born in and through God's love. This makes me a miracle.

I seek and find the face
of God in creation.

Honesty

No legacy is so rich as honesty.
—William Shakespeare

An honest life is my goal. It is not always easy, usually because I'm afraid that if I'm honest then I will not be accepted. John Powell, a Jesuit, wrote a book that explores this theme: *Why Am I Afraid to Tell You Who I Am?* Fear! I'm afraid that if I'm honest, then you will not love me.

But if I'm not honest, if I hide in lies and secrets, can you really love me? No, because I'm not there. When I pretend, the real me becomes invisible. You cannot love what you do not know. Dishonesty keeps me anonymous.

Hence we need honesty. It is the backdrop to our dance in God.

I seek to live an honest life
on a daily basis.

Reality

We don't need more strength or ability or opportunity. What we need is to use what we have.

—Basil S. Walsh

A popular song asked, "Is that all there is?" Yes. And it's enough.

When we *Say Yes to Your Spirit* we are accepting that all we need for happiness, joy, and creativity has been given.

The real question is, are we using what we have been given? I can only speak for myself—in most cases, no. But it's beginning to change. Why? Because I'm realizing that I am enough. Spiritually I am growing in the awareness that not only did God create me but that God is expressed through me. There is a divine quality to my life.

For me, this awareness is relatively new. And it is transformational.

Today I am using what
I have been given.

Growth

The successful man will profit from his mistakes and try again in a different way.

—Dale Carnegie

I learn from my mistakes. Often I grow when I begin to look at what I call mistakes and see them differently: see them as opportunities, gifts that lead to awareness.

Take alcoholism (please!). For years I saw myself as a flawed human being, weak and impaired. Today I'm able to see that my alcoholism is the gateway to understanding obsessive and compulsive behaviors in all areas (not least religion), and it gives me a powerful connection to other human beings. I'm not glad that I'm alcoholic, but I'm glad I know it.

Say Yes to Your Spirit is really about finding our spiritual connection to other human beings and the universe. My awareness of my alcoholism offers such a connection.

In my sobriety
I'm dancing in God.

Love

Once you have learned to love, you will have learned to live.
—Unknown

Love is fascinating. It covers a myriad of feelings: joy, fear, anger, completeness, sadness, ecstasy. Love is life.

Erich Fromm wrote an absorbing book called *The Art of Loving*. Basically what he said is that we need to *learn* to love; it does not come easily. It takes time, patience, and a willingness to see life and God differently.

I used to believe that God not only loves the world but controls it and manipulates it. Now I realize that love is not about control and never about manipulation.

When I was an active alcoholic, my mother said to me, "Leo, I love you enough to let you go." It was the beginning of my recovery. It was the beginning of a new understanding of love: tough love.

My *Say Yes to Your Spirit* involves the complexities of love . . . and it feels good.

Today my love involves letting go.

Dreams

All our dreams can come true, if we have the courage to pursue them.
—Walt Disney

What do I want to be? What do you want to be? And can we see it?

Having dreams is not enough. We need to take the action, or change the attitude, that will make our dreams come true.

Say Yes to Your Spirit is an attitude of mind. Our mind is important because through it we will create the life we wish to live. For many years I thought it was enough to have dreams, but recently I've realized that work and effort are involved in making dreams become a reality. Martin Luther King Jr. said, "You need not only dream. Now is the time to march."

Our dance in God is the action necessary to focus our dreams so that they can become a reality.

I dream with my
feet planted on the ground.

Focus

Never try to teach a pig to sing; it wastes your time and it annoys the pig.

—Paul Dickson

Say Yes to Your Spirit is not a waste of time. Time is not to be wasted. Time is precious.

At a young age, I realized I was not interested in machines. I'm not a practical person. I can change a lightbulb, but that is where my handiwork ends. But I knew I was good with people. I enjoy people, and I can make a connection with most. This awareness has been essential for my life's work and vocation.

What about you? We need to know what talents we have, what we enjoy, what truly interests us, and then focus on developing that passion. Success involves focus and passion.

We rarely are successful at the things we don't enjoy.

I'm focusing on my particular dance.

Reality

A doctor can bury his mistakes, but an architect can only advise his clients to plant vines.
—Frank Lloyd Wright

There is a song that says,

The world still is the same.
You'll never change it.

Some things we can change, and some things are the way they are and will never change. It is important to know this.

We cannot change our parents or the color of our skin or our height. But there are many things that we can change:

- Our attitude.
- The way we treat other people.
- Character defects.
- Our appreciation of other cultures and religions.
- The way we experience God in our lives.

As the Serenity Prayer says, we need to accept the things we cannot change, have the courage to change the things we can, and develop the wisdom to know the difference.

I understand that spirituality is about reality.

Ambition

The indispensable first step to getting the things you want in life is this: decide what you want.
—Ben Stein

For many years I thought that ambition was a negative emotion, something to avoid. I had confused ambition with arrogance. Today we understand that an arrogant person is somebody who would climb the ladder to success by standing on and crushing the lives of others.

Today I understand that ambition is a powerful spiritual attribute that enables achievement. Mother Teresa trusted in God, but she also had ambition. Mahatma Gandhi loved India but also had ambition. Ambition is a necessary step in our dance in God.

I want people to respect the religion and culture of other people. I want people to respect the difference that is essential to God's creation. I'm ambitious to get this message across.

My Say Yes to Your Spirit
involves ambition.

Pride

Give the American people a good cause and there's nothing they can't lick.
—John Wayne

I suppose there is a necessary pride involved in any form of nationalism. I'm a citizen of the United States of America and proud of it. I was born in England, and I'm also proud of my heritage. In our dance in God, confidence and pride are essential. It's hard to dance if we're ashamed.

But there is a toxic form of pride that leads to arrogance, prejudice, and violence. This form of nationalism or religious fervor creates war and division. Spiritually such behavior is anathema.

The respect I have today for my religion and culture enables me to appreciate the pride others have in theirs . . . and it feels good.

I celebrate my heritage.

Hope

Strong hope is a much greater stimulant of life than any single realized joy could be.
—Friedrich W. Nietzsche

Say Yes to Your Spirit is rooted in hope. But what is hope?

For me it is a feeling that God has not only created this world but also is still creating in and through every moment of life. Cocreation means we are encouraged to join God in this creative enterprise and make the world a better place for all of us. I see it happening—sometimes quickly, sometimes slowly, but it is happening.

It is the hope that feeds my optimism and joy. In my dance in God I see the world coming together and divisions being healed . . . hence the smile on my face.

What about you?

Today I have hope and
I affirm joy.

Improvement

Your legacy should be that you made it better than it was when you got it.
—Lee Iacocca

I love to study the lives of artists because I believe that they are always trying to improve the world by their creations. Artists rarely destroy.

This knowledge is important for those of us who wish to *Say Yes to Your Spirit*. We may not be famous, but we are all called to be artists in our particular lives. We can improve the environment, relationships, and international understanding. We can respect animals and express concern toward the poor and homeless. We can make the world a better place.

In Alcoholics Anonymous you hear that service is essential for sobriety. We give to receive. Jesus lived the same message. So did Gautama Buddha. Oh yes, and so can we. Let the dance begin.

Each day I seek to improve my life and in doing so improve the world.

Teamwork

Personal wealth has never been important to me. What is important is the team of people I work with.

—George Davies

"No man is an island," wrote John Donne. We all need each other.

When I was younger I could be a maverick, not sensitive to the needs and concerns of those around me. It wasn't exactly "my way or the highway," but it did verge on arrogance and spiritual snobbery. I'm not proud of those years.

With recovery came teamwork. I couldn't get sober on my own. I needed a partner. I found God and other sober people. Slowly I found Leo.

Teamwork is *Say Yes to Your Spirit*. The more I seek to live the spiritual life, the more I realize it is based upon a connection to others.

Today I'll dance with anyone!

Courage

Courage is resistance to fear, mastery of fear—not absence of fear.
—Mark Twain

I love the word "courage." And I also respect the word "fear."

Jerry Jampolsky said that there are really only two emotions in this world: love and fear. I understand exactly what he is saying, and I agree with him; a part of love is courage.

We should never become prisoners of words. Rather we should always be prepared to be poetic.

Fear is not always a negative word. Fear of water or heights is healthy. Fear of negativity is smart.

As we *Say Yes to Your Spirit* we allow ourselves to dance with words and ideas that can provoke a thought that leads to healing.

I have the courage to dance
with my fears.

April

Style

Style is the dress of thoughts.

—Leo Booth

I was always impressed by the style of Cary Grant. I read somewhere that when he was the young Archie Leach, he saw a man who had great style and began slowly to reinvent himself to become Cary Grant.

I used to be a drunk. I used to be prejudiced. I used to be a sexist. Then, with the help of recovery and spirituality, I reinvented myself . . . with style.

Style is the outward manifestation of our inner spirituality. A song says that you either have it or you don't. I do not agree. Everyone has style. It is our *Say Yes to Your Spirit*. All we need to do is develop it. Are you ready?

I embrace a spiritual style.

Life

The rhythm of life is a powerful beat.
—Dorothy Fields

I've often said that an understanding of spirituality is energy: a positive and creative energy that leads to transformation.

When I do workshops across the country, I often hear participants sharing that they find or discover closeness to God in their encounters with nature, mountains, and the ocean. Recently a participant shared her feelings of vitality while hugging some trees near San Francisco!

Life is all around us. We can connect with the rhythm of life, the universal beat, when we consciously seek to connect with it.

W. H. Davies says it this way:

What is this life if, full of care,
We have no time to stand and stare?

Life really is about connection.

I affirm the rhythm in my life.

Experience

Experience is the name everyone gives to their mistakes.
—Oscar Wilde

Oscar was being a little naughty with this statement. But then again, naughtiness came easily to Oscar!

We do learn from our mistakes. Often in my recovery meetings I share my story and tell some of the mistakes and mishaps in my life, and that usually there is a learning curve associated with these incidents. In the shadow of my life I discover the light!

Also my experience is fed by the stories and incidents that other people share. That's why I love to read. On a daily basis I enrich my experiences by allowing myself to be teachable. You really can teach an old dog new tricks.

Today I gain experience
from my mistakes.

Empathy

If you find it in your heart to care for somebody else, you will have succeeded.
—Maya Angelou

When I was in the presence of my mother, I was always struck by the way she cared for her family, but she also showed empathy with the stranger. My sister is the same. Going shopping with her in the supermarket can take hours because she always finds people to talk with, usually strangers.

I'm a little bit the same. I love people. I enjoy speaking at conferences and churches, seeing faces light up with laughter or struggle with a concept they have not heard before.

Courage and empathy contribute to the rhythm in life we call love. *Say Yes to Your Spirit* is essentially about love: love of God, love of self, love of others.

I care because I've been cared for.

Failure

You may be disappointed if you fail, but you are doomed if you don't try.
—Beverly Sills

Some friends of mine have recently shared that the reason they feel that they've not been successful in their lives is fear of failure. This has included relationships. This fear of being rejected stopped them from asking a particular man or woman out on a date. Is this crazy? Yes. But true.

I really agree with Beverly Sills, because everybody experiences aspects of life that don't work out for them. I'm not sure I'd call it failure, but the process of trying is a learning experience in itself. Also concerning relationships, the worst that can happen is that they say, "No." So, if you're smart, you fish in another part of the lake!

Say Yes to Your Spirit always involves risk. And remember: you don't always have to keep doing what you've done!

My dance in God includes risk.

Suffering

Every flower must grow through dirt.
—Author Unknown

Say Yes to Your Spirit is about divinity, love, and beauty, but it also includes suffering.

Nobody is going to get out of life alive, and nobody leaves this life without experiencing pain and suffering. My suffering, although not exhaustively, has been from alcoholism; for others it can be divorce, poverty, racism, sexual abuse, sickness—the list is endless. We all suffer in life.

But suffering is not the whole story. If we are to move away from victimization, we need to accept this and be prepared to move on. Day follows night; after the rain comes sunshine; better days inevitably follow.

Just as the dirt is essential to the flower, so is suffering essential in the molding of the spiritual life.

I thank God for the dirt
I can dust away.

Motivation

Motivation will almost always beat mere talent.

—Norman R. Augustine

When you begin to realize that *Say Yes to Your Spirit* is about understanding that God is present within each and every one of us, this awareness becomes the motivation to create success in our lives. Our dance in God is a dance of joy and confidence, with unlimited potential for facing any difficulties.

I've said earlier in this book that the notion of co-creation, putting our hand in the hand of God, moves us away from waiting for blessings; now we know that we can create them. It is truly transformational.

Alcoholism, depression, and financial insecurity can all be overcome if we are prepared to make the necessary changes in our life. The act of seeking help and moving into a positive attitude are the key ingredients to success.

The dance begins when we are prepared to move from apathy to optimism.

I am motivated to improve my life.

Imagination

Imagination is the highest kite one can fly.
—Lauren Bacall

It's always dangerous to make reference to a movie in meditations; however, recently I saw the movie *Finding Neverland* with Johnny Depp and Kate Winslet. I believe that it will be popular for years, so if you haven't seen it I suggest renting it.

It is about James Barrie, the writer who created *Peter Pan*. It embraces the concept of imagination. If you can see something wonderful in your mind, then you can change your feelings about life. It is a feel-good movie that helps us think optimistically about remaining young at heart, confronting sickness, and moving into death. And it is assuredly spiritual.

We dance in God when we give ourselves permission to play in life.

I'm polishing God's gift
of imagination.

Force

Not everything that is forced can be changed, but nothing can be changed until it is forced.
—James Baldwin

It's unusual to have a meditation that discusses force. But force is a reality. Every day of our lives we are dealing with pressures—some good, some not so good.

- The pressure to find employment or improve our finances.
- The pressure to deal with an awkward relationship.
- The pressure to go see the doctor about a pain that has been nagging us for months.
- The pressure about what to do in retirement.

Pressure and force are aspects of life that are ever present but rarely discussed. Today we will face them.

I accept the necessary pressures that are in my life.

Commitment

Be like a postage stamp. Stick to one thing until you get there.
—Josh Billings

Do one thing at a time. The journey begins with the first step: first things first.

Many statements support the conviction that achievement and success come from a solid commitment, staying focused. In recovery from addiction many people have been helped by a 12-step program. And it is emphasized that you do the program one step at a time, following the order in which the steps are written!

The enemy of the *Say Yes to Your Spirit* philosophy is chaos—doing things higgledy-piggledy, not being focused. Staying with the analogy of dance, it's important to know the steps and suggested glides. Otherwise you and your partner can find yourselves in a horrible heap on the floor. Nasty!

Today I face life one step at a time.

Character

Character may be manifested in the great moments, but it is made in the small ones.
—Phillip Brooks

Say Yes to Your Spirit is really finding God or a Higher Power in the everyday experiences of life, the small incidents that other people can miss. These little things add up to be the creative ingredients of character.

- Remembering to say "hello" to friends and strangers as you pass through your busy day.
- Picking up somebody else's trash that has been left on the street.
- Remembering to invite a lonely person to your Thanksgiving or Christmas meal.
- Giving flowers to your loved one for no reason other than they express your love.
- Remembering to write a thank-you note for a gift received in the mail.

These small moments make our dance in God enjoyable.

Today I understand that little things mean a lot.

Vision

Shoot for the moon. Even if you miss, you'll land among the stars.
—Les Brown

I've always felt that spirituality and imagination are intertwined. To be able to see the big picture while living our own particular life is the essence of *Say Yes to Your Spirit.*

I think I experienced this when I changed the theme of this book from "dancing with God" to "dancing in God." Something about living *in* God and God's creative powers living *in* us takes us one step further along the spiritual path than simply being *with* God.

The phrase "dancing in God" also emphasizes the powers of imagination and vision that enable us to demonstrate incredible feats in our lives. With this awareness we are able to create new ideas about spirituality, new ways of writing about revelation, a new understanding of our daily dance in God.

Wow. I'm excited already.

I'm shooting for the moon
and the stars.

Growth

It's never too late to be what you might have been.

—George Eliot

I was sitting recently with a friend who was very depressed because he felt that he had achieved nothing in his life. He kept pointing out the wonderful things that I had achieved and what I was continuing to do with my life, like writing this book.

Then I gently pointed out to him that he was at least twenty years younger than me and, oh yes, he had done some wonderful things already in his life. He was allowing himself to become depressed because he was forgetting the future; *tomorrow is another day.*

Optimism is based upon having a positive view, not only for today, but also for tomorrow.

We both sat and thought about what he truly had achieved in his life, and we also envisioned for his future.

He left with a smile on his face.

My Say Yes to Your Spirit *is based upon a better tomorrow.*

Ideas

An idea is salvation by imagination.

—Frank Lloyd Wright

I had this idea about writing a book that was for everyone. Sure, recovering alcoholics and drug addicts, and therapists who work in my professional field would read it, but it should also be for everyone.

I knew it would be about spirituality, but a cocreative spirituality that revolved around the idea of dance: dancing in God, taking our Higher Power into our lives, but more than this, celebrating the Spirit that was given; it is already here!

The result is what you are reading. A certain imagination is necessary to write 366 meditations, but as I look around at life, I realize the book wrote itself.

I thank God for the gift of imagination.

Reputation

You can't build a reputation on what you are going to do.
—Henry Ford

In the recovery from addiction movement we hear a great deal about procrastination. It is a generalization, but often it appears that the addict suffers from putting things off, almost like a symptom of the disease. Naturally a reputation would suffer if this behavior is allowed to continue.

Say Yes to Your Spirit is about facing life as it is, taking responsibility for those things that need to change. In most cases we can change those things about our life that we don't like or that are hurting us. This is what dancing in God is all about; we have the spiritual power to overcome most obstacles.

Those of us who choose to live *Say Yes to Your Spirit* will eventually get a reputation for being caring, loving, and responsible.

I'm concerned about what
you think about me.

Perseverance

He who limps is still walking.

—Stanislaw J. Lec

I love this quotation. It is so visual and thought provoking. In my mind I can actually see a person limping up a dusty pathway.

Often in writing *Say Yes to Your Spirit* I've found the need to use metaphors and poetry to paint a picture. In the concept of dancing in God, I can actually see me dancing with God, who happens to look like the traditional pictures of Jesus, and I am gliding along with a smile on my face. Obviously I'm quite a good dancer because Jesus is smiling too!

The limp in the quotation signifies the challenges that we all must face in life. But these challenges rarely stop us in our tracks. Most times we are able to overcome them or learn to live with them. That takes perseverance—a gift that God has given us.

Are we using this gift?

The times I catch myself limping
I remember I am still walking.

Excellence

Whatever you are, be a good one.
—Abraham Lincoln

The world is made up of a variety of people with a variety of gifts and cultural insights. *Say Yes to Your Spirit* celebrates this God-given fact of life.

I suppose that the reason some people are not able to celebrate who they are or what they are is because of a commingling of guilt and shame.

This is the reason that so many of my readers are in, what is politely called, "recovery." They are healing, on a daily basis, from something or someone who created their low self-esteem. As a result, what Abraham Lincoln said in the quote is easier said than realized. It will take effort, possibly therapy, and an understanding of spirituality that proclaims a God who is involved in our lives to be the best that we can be.

Excellence in living can only come when we respect and love ourselves and others.

I am good at what I do.

Courage

Courage is the price that life exacts for granting peace.
—Amelia Earhart

How true this saying is. Whatever peace has been achieved in this world has been created by men and women who have shown great courage. Not only did they risk their lives, but many gave their lives for the cause they championed. Along the way they also suffered ostracism and persecution.

But they could do no other. This is the physical reality of *Say Yes to Your Spirit*. It is the lived-out drama of what it means to dance in God. And the world has changed.

Racism, sexism, homophobia, witch burning, slavery, and many more exploitations have shriveled in the world, although they have not been completely obliterated, because great men and women showed courage.

Celebrate the power of the heavenly Spirit.

I affirm courage in my life.

Liberty

Life without liberty is like a body without spirit.
—Kahlil Gibran

I suppose one of the most important qualities of life is liberty, also known as freedom: the concept of saying and doing what you want and when you want, as long as you are not knowingly hurting somebody else.

Spirituality is about proclaiming this liberty. Earlier I've said that I don't want to live in a religious box. Let us be clear; religious addiction and religious abuse exist. In the name of God, some people are hurt, maligned, ridiculed, and in extreme cases killed by religious people who feel they have a right to judge and condemn. This unfortunately is still happening in some parts of the world.

Spirituality seeks to bring people together with a sincere respect for each others' religions and cultures. Spirituality is the key that opens the religious box.

I affirm a freedom that is inclusive.

Adventure

Do not follow where the path may lead. Go instead where there is no path and leave a trail.
—Ralph Waldo Emerson

Dare to be different. Dare to journey where no man or woman has gone before: the adventure of the individual.

I remember hearing that unity is not the same as uniformity. When we are in unity with one another, we can still celebrate diversity and respect individuality. With this concept as a foundation, people are able to create original artwork, explore new fantasies, and write and produce plays that challenge society in a completely different way. We all benefit.

Adventure does not exist without the freedom to tread a path that has never been traveled.

I will surely meet some of you as I tread the road of happy destiny.

Individuality

Be who you are and say what you feel, because those who mind don't matter and those who matter don't mind.

—Dr. Seuss

Being an individual is very hard. I catch myself frequently trying to please the crowd at the expense of saying or doing what I believe is right.

This saying of Dr. Seuss is offered to make us think, but it tends to be a generalization. Those who do mind also matter; indeed a life lived without healthy criticism would not be intellectually fertile. Also those who are important to our life are not always going to give us a pass.

However, we can't always please everyone, and in our dance in God some people will choose to sit it out!

I am an individual and a member of society.

Generosity

Generosity is the flower of justice.
—Nathaniel Hawthorne

S*ay Yes to Your Spirit* involves generosity. It is really important to give, not simply money—although money is important and should be shared—but also to give of oneself.

Optimism is part of my understanding of generosity. I believe it to be spiritually important to be both positive and creative, which affects my attitude and behavior.

Today I'm willing to give my time and money to a cause that I deem to be important. An example is recovery from alcoholism. I will often travel to other countries to share my strength and hope with those who are still struggling. And I do this for no honorarium. What have I discovered by doing this? Well, when I'm generous I receive back a hundredfold.

I've discovered my generosity is spiritually rewarding.

Balance

We make a living by what we get, but we make a life by what we give.

—Norman MacEwan

A word that is often used in discussing spirituality is balance. In Asia this is often described as discovering the yin and yang of life: perfect harmony.

For any successful life we need to be able to give and receive, to make and also to take. Responsibility always shadows balance because it stresses the need for us to be accountable for the life we live; indeed, we have a duty to pay our dues. Family, mortgage, living expenses all need to be paid for, so in this sense we shouldn't ever "give away the farm." At the same time it is important for our spiritual life to share with others, especially those in need.

Today I'm able to live this balance.

Spiritually I sacrifice
what makes sense.

Happiness

Most people ask for happiness on condition. Happiness can only be felt if you don't set any conditions.

—Arthur Rubinstein

For too many years I lived with conditions.

- I will do this if you do that.
- I'll be your friend if you do this for me.
- I really love you, God, but this is what I want.
- I will stop drinking if I get the following. . . .

Then I read about letting go and enjoying the moment for what it is. No conditions. My life improved, and I felt happier.

I dance in God on a daily basis,
and I have no expectations.

Choice

Choice, not chance, determines one's destiny.
—Author Unknown

Over the years I've come to consider choice a valuable spiritual word. It is my acknowledgment of choice that has energized my understanding of cocreation.

I choose to place my hand in the hand of God. I do believe that God's hand is extended toward me, but I must grab it. It is my choice. If I do not grab the hand of God, or determine not to take the necessary steps in my dance in God, then nothing happens . . . or nothing creative happens.

Spiritually this approach can be very scary; we can choose to destroy our lives. We can choose to remain unhappy. We can choose to stay drunk.

I affirm that I play a powerful role in my cocreative dance in God.

Intelligence

Many people have intelligence. Few have common sense.
—Winston Churchill

Kevin Taylor, a friend who is an Episcopal priest, often says, "I'm afraid he is lacking common sense." At times he has made this statement about me!

He is right. A person can be intelligent, educated, and an avid reader and watcher of the History Channel . . . and yet lack common sense. Brilliant people can still make irresponsible choices.

Say Yes to Your Spirit embraces the practical side of life.

- Be careful with money.
- Choose healthy friendships.
- Avoid destructive behaviors.
- Know when we need to change our attitude.

Common sense adds music to our dance.

Today I seek the gift of common sense.

Education

Education is not preparation for life; education is life itself.

—John Dewey

Descartes said, "Cogito ergo sum." I think, therefore I am.

Education is not just about school, books, and attaining a degree. It is about observing life. Jesus said, "Having eyes, don't you see? Having ears, don't you hear?" (Mark 8:18)

I often develop my educational gifts of insight and intuition by observing people, really looking at them: how they walk, dress, speak . . . and especially their faces. The eyes have often been called the window of the soul. Seeing a person's eyes can tell you so much.

Nature, visiting other countries, experiencing different cultures all add to our education in life.

Today I understand that
I am a student of life.

Artists

Every artist dips his brush in his own soul and paints his own nature into his pictures.
—Henry Ward Beecher

I love biographies. I love reading about the lives of famous actors, painters, musicians, even politicians.

Greatness often seemed to be accompanied by suffering, misunderstanding, and the occasional scandal, which makes for a great read.

I think that *Say Yes to Your Spirit* is about developing the artistic side of our nature that we all have. Indeed we couldn't appreciate the movies or shows that are performed without being able to identify with the characters, especially the suffering.

Where is the creativity in your soul? Maybe it is your choice of music, or the way you dress, or the car you drive. Artistry is all around us, and it reflects who we are.

I affirm my artistry
on a daily basis.

Ignorance

If you think education is expensive, try ignorance.
—Derek Bok

I took a group of people to China a few years ago. I remember that one of the group members came to me and said that she really liked the temples and countryside, but why did we have to eat "foreign food"? I tried to explain that Chinese food is not foreign to the people living in China.

Ignorance is the enemy of living the spiritual life because it tends to degrade, shame, and discount other people, countries, languages, and religions. Ignorance has created terrible suffering. Think of how many women were condemned as witches in the name of religion because they kept a cat or lived alone. How many scientists were persecuted for saying that the Earth is round? To dance in God we must have an open mind for new and challenging solutions.

I seek God with the help of
a healthy education.

Appreciation

The music is nothing if the audience is deaf.

—Walter Lippmann

Say Yes to Your Spirit is about having an open mind. A character flaw that I seek to overcome on a daily basis is contempt prior to investigation. Sometimes I have a feeling about something that is not based on any evidence . . . *and I'm wrong.*

- For years I never wanted to go to Germany because I imagined it to be a gloomy, dirty, industrialized country. When I eventually went to Germany I found a most beautiful countryside and wonderful people.
- I said that French food was too rich and saucy. Then I tried it. It was exquisite.
- I said that brown shoes were unprofessional. Then I bought a pair and liked them.

Metaphysically I need to open my ears. Only then will I hear the music.

Today I seek experience before making a judgment.

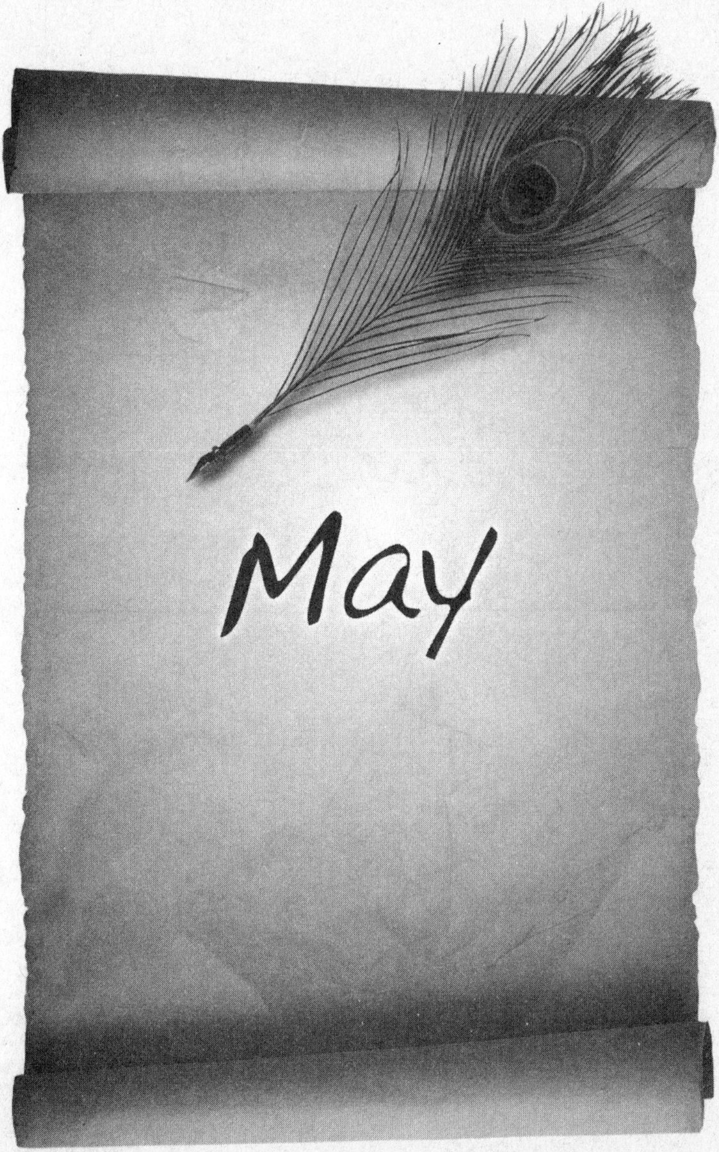
May

Spirituality

Spirituality is a choice to step outside the religious box.
—Leo Booth

I'm not so religious that I cannot appreciate the problems that so many people have with religion. When somebody says that they are agnostic or atheist it usually implies that:

- They have a genuine disagreement with a religious theory or viewpoint,

or

- They have been hurt by a religion, felt rejection, and react by separating themselves from all religions.

When we step outside the religious box we appreciate the variety of spiritual experience and the wounds caused by religious abuse.

Today I dance with you because
I simply love you.

Respect

"Silent" and "listen" are spelled with the same letters.

—Unknown

I remember somebody once saying to me, "You don't have to say anything. Just listen to me."

A form of respect can only be discovered in silence. Only then can we really hear what God or anybody else is saying to us.

The psalmist says, "Be still and know that I am God." In the silence we hear the music of life, and when we hear the music we are able to dance the dance of Spirit.

I have learned that spiritual people often have around them an atmosphere of silence; they are gentle people, and this interior silence breeds a special kind of respect.

I seek to develop silence as I nurture my ability to listen.

Art

Art is life.

—Michelangelo

Thank God that in language we have so much choice, diversity, and different ways to say the same thing. It stops this book from being boring!

Say Yes to Your Spirit is saying what Michelangelo is saying in the above statement. Art is really about being creative, living rather than suffocating, seeking freedom rather than staying in a religious box. Artists always embrace the energy that reverberates in life, and they seek to reflect it.

So, life is art, essentially. We seek to live the spiritual life when we are affirming the artist who exists in each of us . . . and the artist is waiting to dance.

My art is my life.

Childlike

The child in me wants to play.

—Charlie Chaplin

I always enjoyed Charlie Chaplin. Even when he didn't seem to be doing anything he could make me laugh. And he reflected innocence. A part of him was forever the child. That is what made him so very attractive.

I have that quality. You have that quality. And it is delightful . . . attractive.

Why do so few people reveal this quality in their lives? Why are so many people so serious? What stops people from playing? Probably fear. We think that adults are expected to be serious. Also, many of us do not recognize that the child from our childhood is still present in our lives, and so many of us had a wounded childhood.

It is time to be aware, time to heal . . . time to dance.

I will allow the child in me to play.

Fear

We fear things in proportion to our ignorance of them.

—Titus Livius

We've read already in these meditations that there are really only two emotions in life: fear and love.

Usually I fear what I do not understand, yet when I take time to understand it, even if I don't agree with it, I'm able to accept it.

I wrote a book called *The Wisdom of Letting Go,* in which I said that most violence, prejudice, religious intolerance, and sexism were rooted in fear. It follows that our *Say Yes to Your Spirit* must involve a willingness to educate ourselves about people who are different. I've reconciled myself to the fact that I will be forever a student of life. This really is my dance in God. And I'm learning to live with and enjoy diversity.

I'm healing my fears through education.

Prosperity

The past does not equal the future.

—Anthony Robbins

I used to think that if I was a good person I would be prosperous. God would see to it! When I say "a good person," I really meant going to church, saying my prayers, respecting my parents, and obeying my elders.

I've only recently come to understand that prosperity requires my involvement: cocreation. Indeed, I create my future, and if we understand that prosperity is more than simply money, and we include happiness, work, enjoyment of others, and personal satisfaction in life, then the choices we make about what we do with our lives become paramount.

In a sense the past is spent; the future, however, is what we want to make of it. This is exciting. It is also the foundation of *Say Yes to Your Spirit*.

Today I'm personally involved in my prosperity.

Thoughts

Think big thoughts, but relish small pleasures.

—H. Jackson Brown Jr.

I've just been scratching between my toes . . . and I love it.

I had a salted boiled egg for breakfast . . . and I really enjoyed it.

In two hours I'm going to walk along the beach, take off my shoes and socks, paddle in the ocean . . . and I can't wait.

They are small pleasures, but important.

Say Yes to Your Spirit is not just about lofty ideals but the recognition and importance of the small things in life that make life worth living.

Nature calls; yet another pleasure!

I keep my feet on the ground when
I look to see the stars.

Understanding

Peace cannot be kept by force. It can only be achieved by understanding.
—Albert Einstein

I have recently caught myself saying that if I really understood you and what made you tick, I could never hate you. I believe this. Understanding is the key to relationship and love.

When Albert Einstein said that peace cannot be kept by force, he affirmed what many people around the world came to realize in their relationship with Iraq. Yes, we needed to remove the tyrant. Yes, we needed to remove the governmental dictatorship, but peace could only be achieved by understanding the mind and culture of an ancient people. As I write, the tensions in Iraq have not been resolved.

As with countries, so with people; peace can only be achieved by respect that is based on understanding.

Understanding and respect are key steps in my dance in God.

Achievement

What the mind of man can conceive and believe, it can achieve.
—Napoleon Hill

If you can see it, you can be it.

I'm really interested in visioning: seeing something in my mind and then making choices to bring it into reality.

- I've done this with my appearance.
- I've done this with the rooms in my house.
- I've done this with vacations and visits to England.
- I've done this with the development of significant friendships.

I believe that we share in the Mind of God. And because I believe in a Creator God, indeed a God who is still creating in the universe, then I believe that we also can create.

Jesus said, "Having eyes do you not see?" (Mark 8:18)

Today I'm able to see where I am going in my life . . . and it is fun.

I see that God is inviting me to dance.

Sharing

The secret to life is to share.

—Kien Lam

Kien Lam is my office manager. Often when we are having lunch together he will offer me some of his food: a piece of pork or chicken, some rice, a portion of his orange.

Kien enjoys sharing.

We cannot *Say Yes to Your Spirit* when we are unwilling to share what we have been given. In the sharing is the love.

When we are prepared to dance in God we are also prepared to share the space; dancing is the movement of respect.

Today I enjoy sharing conversation, food, money, and dreams. And when I share I become more alive, more involved, more real . . . more!

Do you share your life?

Sharing is part of my spiritual awakening.

Money

The love of money is the root of all evil.
—1 Timothy 6:10

We can be obsessed with anything. We can be compulsive around sex, gambling, people, alcohol, drugs, work . . . and also money.

Money is not evil, bad, or sinful. But it can be dangerous if it is not used.

Jesus reinforced this observation in a parable about a fearful steward, suggesting that money should be invested. Money is creative. It can bring work, joy, happiness, travel, security . . . but it can also make us very unhappy.

How do we dance with money? Don't make it into more than it is, but appreciate all that it can create.

Today I respect the power of money.

Strategy

We will attack Aqaba from the back; from the desert.

—T. E. Lawrence

We sometimes need to be willing to think differently, occasionally daringly.

No army had ever crossed the Nefud Desert before, and so the guns that defended the Port of Aqaba were facing the sea. Lawrence of Arabia took a risk. He dared to take an army and do what had never been done before, and he was successful.

Say Yes to Your Spirit sometimes involves taking a risk—maybe doing what you have never done before. It requires a willingness to think differently. Greatness often comes at a price.

Am I willing to take a risk?

Today I am willing to educate myself so that I can take sensible risks.

Manners

Good manners will open doors that the best education cannot.

—Clarence Thomas

My father always made sure that my mother walked on the inside as they walked down the street. Old-fashioned protection!

Mother said that conversation should be like tennis; no one person should be doing all the talking.

My sister often reminds me that a kindness does not need to be spoken about. Do it . . . and move on.

Manners make for a good character, and they necessarily contribute to *Say Yes to Your Spirit*.

Our dance in God requires manners, gentleness, space, and personal respect.

Today I seek to nurture good manners in my life.

Diversity

All races and religions: that's America to me.

—Earl Robinson

Say Yes to Your Spirit is really about not only accepting diversity but celebrating it.

We grow spiritually not just *in* our differences but *because* of our differences, and I believe that the God-given diversity that makes up this world tells us something about God: the one and the many.

For years I thought there was one way of understanding the Bible, one way to worship God, one path to heaven, one true religion. Today I do not believe this.

I believe there are many ways of understanding the Bible, many ways to worship God, many paths to heaven, many true and noble religions.

The dance has many steps.

I am richer for the diversity
that is in my world.

Effort

The reward of a thing well done is to have done it.

—Ralph Waldo Emerson

Thinking about what you want to do does not achieve it. Talking about your hopes and dreams in itself does not make them happen. Words and ideas are not substitutes for action.

Since I've become a Unity minister of Christianity I've been directed to contemplate the word "cocreation." It is the spiritual effort that enables achievement. God may want something to happen in the world, but a response from us is required. I'm reminded that Dr. Martin Luther King Jr. said to his congregation that they needed to do more than pray for freedom. They needed to also march. Effort is the willingness to put your body where your mouth is.

That really is *Say Yes to Your Spirit.*

Are you saying it?

Today I'm ready to activate my belief.

Art

A picture is a poem without words.
—Horace

There are many ways to present an idea and the use of language, words, is probably the most common. We communicate what we think or believe in short- or long-winded sentences, where the medium is newspapers, novels, textbooks, or text messages. (I add this because I've just learned today how to send a text message, and I'm so pleased with myself!)

But let us not forget the artist. With paint from a brush, an artist is able to reveal glory, misery, forgiveness, and hope.

In one picture frame we can see so many stories; all that is required is our imagination.

Poetry is a picture set to words. But it is not unlike prose. There is not necessarily only one meaning to the poem; again each person's imagination is required. All the above are varieties of our dance in God.

Art is my spiritual nourishment.

Freedom

Let freedom reign. The sun never set on so glorious a human achievement.
—Nelson Mandela

Freedom often comes at a price. Nelson Mandela was willing to pay that price. For many people he is a saint. He's certainly a hero—brave, noble, and committed.

I sometimes take freedom for granted. I've lived my life in democracy. I've always had a vote. I never experienced racial or sexual prejudice, never knew real poverty, and never went a day without food available to me.

Freedom is a blessing, and I've been blessed. But with this gift comes a challenge: am I prepared to carry the message of freedom to those who are still suffering oppression? Yes.

How? By the philosophy that is the foundation of *Say Yes to Your Spirit*. It is for everyone. It seeks to affirm the value of all life. It really is the message of freedom.

Today I know that freedom is life;
oppression is existence.

Patience

Patience is the art of hoping.
—Luc de Clapier de Vauvanarques

I used to be so impatient, especially when I was drinking alcohol: my way or the highway, hurry up, move along, be quicker, *rush*. . . .

Today I have patience. Well, not every day, but most days. Thomas Hardy suggests that patience is really about hoping—hoping that things will get better, that things work out in the end, that often when we let go, things fall into place.

Yes, all that is true. And I think that patience involves a gentle acceptance; we are not God. It's okay to wait for what we want. I need to respect the time schedule of others. Tomorrow is another day.

Say Yes to Your Spirit includes all the above . . . and what has not been said!

Today I can sit out a dance,
and that's okay.

Expression

Of all the things you wear, your expression is the most important.
—Author Unknown

My understanding of spirituality has always included how we express ourselves, not only mentally, but also physically.

I remember once doing a church service when I asked the congregation, "Are you happy?" They didn't seem to know. Then somebody yelled out, "Yes. We're happy." I looked at them for a moment and then said, "Tell your face. Because your face doesn't seem to know that you are happy!"

I believe that our faces are very important. How do we express ourselves? There does not seem to be much point in having a positive attitude if it doesn't reveal itself in our expression.

Say Yes to Your Spirit is about expressing our whole selves, including the face.

Today I'm dancing with
a smile on my face.

Decisions

The hardest thing in life is to learn which bridge to cross and which to burn.

—Laurence J. Peter

I sometimes hear people say, "Let go and let God!" I know what they mean, but I must not take this literally or I'll be in a mess. Somebody said at a meeting I attended in the early morning, "Don't think. Get out of your own way." People applauded. I know what he meant, but I don't think you should take such admonitions literally.

Say Yes to Your Spirit is about being responsible. I know I am not responsible for you, but I am responsible for me. And I need to make decisions.

I certainly don't want to play God, but I need to play Leo.

I'm not the dance, but I'm an important part of the dance. Today I know this.

Thank you for the gift of choice.

Self-Discipline

Self-discipline is when your conscience tells you to do something and you don't talk back.
—W. K. Hope

I've always admired friends who get up early in the morning and go for a run. I admire even more those who regularly attend the gym, regardless of weather or holidays. Ah, Tuesday . . . must be gym day!

Exercise does not come easily to me. I prefer dieting over running. Carrying a few extra pounds does not make me depressed.

But I do have self-discipline when it comes to work, especially writing. I've said many times that it's easier to learn from a teacher whom we like; also it's easier to practice self-discipline if you like what you need to do. You see, I really enjoy writing. *Say Yes to Your Spirit* is about excelling in what you like.

Thank God we don't all like the same things!

I've found the dance that I enjoy.

Friendship

A real friend is one who walks in when the rest of the world walks out.
—Walter Winchell

We all have those days and weeks when things are not going well. Winston Churchill called them "the days of the black dog." I've had such days often—when I feel lost, depressed, alone, fearful, and absolutely spent.

Thank God for friends. And it's great if you are able to find a few friends in your family!

Friends seem to know when you are isolating. They call, inviting you out for dinner or suggesting a movie.

They know when you are fearful, and they quietly support you, offering a gentle but hopeful word of comfort.

Friends *know*, and that allows you to be known.

My friends really are my family.

My Say Yes to Your Spirit
involves friendship.

Questions

The most important thing is to not stop questioning.
—Albert Einstein

When I was younger I would always be asking questions, usually irritating the teacher or priest.

- Why are we told that only people who accept Jesus will go to heaven? It doesn't seem very fair to the non-Christian.
- If Adam and Eve were the first people on Earth and they had two sons, who did the sons marry?
- If the church was wrong about the world being flat, couldn't they be wrong about other things?
- If people are born gay, isn't God responsible?

As you can imagine, some people got really frustrated with me. I was shamed for asking too many questions, and for years I remained silent.

Today I'm asking questions again.

God gave me a brain to use.

Extraordinary

Extraordinary claims require extraordinary evidence.
—Carl Sagan

Say Yes to Your Spirit is an adventure into the extraordinary. When we understand that we have unlimited possibilities, and that we can change the way we say and do things, then a new world awaits us.

The challenge is letting go of the old ideas, the old model, to enter the world of the extraordinary. An example is the model I use for spirituality. For years people tended to talk about a human being having a mental, physical, and spiritual aspect; when we use this model, however, we have separated the spiritual from the mental and physical.

I've suggested that a human being comprises mental, physical, and emotional attributes, and they are *all* spiritual. Our minds are spiritual. Our bodies are spiritual. Our emotions are spiritual. This approach gives a holistic understanding of being human that leads to extraordinary possibilities.

I embrace the possibilities of the extraordinary on a daily basis.

Humor

Don't let worry kill you. Let the church help.

—Author Unknown

It would be almost impossible to *Say Yes to Your Spirit* without having a sense of humor. I suppose at the core of having a sense of humor is humility—not taking yourself too seriously.

When I was in active addiction with my drinking, I took everything in life in a serious and pompous manner—and created havoc. Today I relax. When I feel a need for a gentle laugh, I take my clothes off and look in the mirror!

But seriously, I do believe an insight into spirituality is not only to look on the brighter side of life but also to find the humor in everyday living.

Today I dance in God with
a smile on my face.

Politeness

Rudeness is the weak man's imitation of strength.
—Eric Hoffer

I think spirituality includes being polite: treating people with respect, affording each person the dignity we would like shown to us.

Why would a person be rude? I'm sure we could think up many reasons, but my personal experience with rude people is that they are insecure. They have a fear of others that they compensate for with aggression, and this world seems to be drowning in acts of violence.

The remedy is to teach politeness . . . ordinary kindness. This is what *Say Yes to Your Spirit* is about: treating people with the same love and respect that we would like to experience.

You cannot dance in God if you are arguing!

When I am occasionally rude,
I seek to apologize as quickly as possible.

Love

Love is never having to say you're sorry.

—Erich Segal, Love Story

I think this is a poetic saying, and I like the concept that in a loving relationship there is an intuition that really understands the other person. You know that they really do not mean to hurt or offend you. You know.

Poetically I can understand this; however, there are times when we all need to say we are sorry for what we have said or done. We especially need to apologize to the people whom we love. Forgiveness is based on being sorry.

Say Yes to Your Spirit is embracing the diversity and difference that exist in this world. At times there will be disagreements and confrontations. A clash of opinions and personalities is inevitable. We will all, at times, need to say "Sorry."

Today I understand that love and forgiveness are intertwined.

Prayer

I pray, not to change God but to change myself.

—C. S. Lewis

I was raised to believe that if I pray hard enough, long enough, and often enough, then maybe, just maybe, God would hear my prayer and grant my request.

- Prayer was about getting God's attention.
- Prayer was about making my request.
- Prayer was rooted in God's grace being bestowed upon me.

And then I waited!

With the help of teachers like C. S. Lewis I began to realize that prayer also involved me. Did I hear my prayers? Was I willing to do the hard work that might be involved in attaining my request? Would I be willing to change?

Say Yes to Your Spirit is celebrating and acknowledging my involvement in God's creativity.

I am truly ready to walk my prayer.

Integrity

Few are those who see with their own eyes and feel with their own hearts.
—Albert Einstein

For many years I've battled with being a people pleaser. I try to figure out what you want me to do or say, and then I do it. This behavior rarely makes me happy, but it satisfies you. Often when I want to be liked or accepted, the focus is on pleasing people. I don't like this aspect of my behavior, and I'm trying to change it.

How? I am developing my personal integrity. I need to know what I think and share it, even if you don't agree. I need to know what I think is the right thing to do and do it, even if you would have me do something different.

Say Yes to Your Spirit is about becoming your own person.

I'm seeking to develop integrity in my spiritual life.

Respect

Treat other people the way you would like to be treated.

—Golden Rule (and from many other faith traditions)

I believe what in our culture is known as the Golden Rule is the key to living *Say Yes to Your Spirit*. I do not believe it is difficult, but it requires remembering to do it. I need to remember that I need to live a spiritual life, which includes the following values:

- Love
- Respect
- Acceptance
- Forgiveness

If people around me treat me with these values in mind, I can more easily be what I believe God would want me to be. If this is true for me, it is also true for you.

Am I willing to give you what I know that I need?

The Golden Rule makes sense for me and the world.

Discipleship

Follow me.

—Jesus

These two words changed the world.

Say Yes to Your Spirit seeks to include all the great rel gions and philosophies that have been promulgated i this world, and the teachings of Jesus have had a might influence for good.

But the above statement requires a response from us Are we willing to follow? Obviously the statement does not mean to literally "follow," but rather to accept and absorb the teachings of Jesus.

I've said throughout this book that our relationship with God is a dance; we have steps to make . . . steps that only we can make.

We need to take a realistic look at our lives and ask, "What are my spiritual goals?"

"Follow me" requires self-examination.

I want to follow the path of truth.

June

Spirituality

For me, spirituality is best summed up in being a positive and creative person.

—Leo Booth

Some years ago I was searching for a definition of spirituality because I knew that it was an important ingredient in the healing process. I began to think about my own alcoholism; it has the effect of making the sufferer negative, and always there are the symptoms of being destructive and negative. Then I realized that spirituality was about the opposite: being positive and creative.

I have found this definition to be helpful in my life, not only as a person recovering from alcoholism, but also by helping me develop healthier attitudes and behaviors.

This is my foundation for *Say Yes to Your Spirit*.

I seek, on a daily basis, to be a positive and creative human being.

Wonder

Men love to wonder, and that is the seed of science.
—Ralph Waldo Emerson

Say Yes to Your Spirit takes us into the world of wonderment: so much to see, so much to experience, so much to hear and appreciate.

Science plays an important part in the world of wonderment, but so do art, music, poetry, therapy, business, finance . . . and the ordinary events that happen in our daily lives:

- Enjoying a meal with friends.
- Watching children play on the beach.
- Experiencing wildlife in a forest.
- Expressing sexually in a loving relationship.

My experience is that if we do not feel the gift of wonder, we can so easily become depressed.

Depression is the enemy of the spiritual life.

I dance with a sense of wonder.

Failure

No man is a failure who is enjoying life.
—William Faulkner

I really enjoy my life. I enjoy recovery. I enjoy my work. I enjoy visiting many parts of America and the world. I really enjoy food. I enjoy . . . period.

Do I get depressed? Yes, but not for long. I seek to carry within myself a message of gratitude and always I have happy songs in my mind. When I'm feeling blah, I sing a song or hum a tune, call a friend, or eat some cheese. The blah cannot survive good brie!

I do not give energy to thoughts of failure. I'm not an egomaniac, but I remember my achievements. And I smile.

I seek a daily life of enjoyment.

Beauty

Beauty is not caused. It is.

—Emily Dickinson

Say Yes to Your Spirit is consciously seeing beauty all around me, especially in the ordinary events of life:

- The preparation of an orange at lunchtime.
- The clothes I select to go to the office.
- The faces of the people on the street, especially children going to school.
- The palm tree swaying on the sidewalk.
- The shape of the clouds in the sky.

Beauty is all around me. Today I'm able to see it.

Thank you for the beauty in this world.

Laughter

You grow up the day you have your first real laugh at yourself.
—Ethel Barrymore

I caught a glimpse of myself in the mirror after a shower, and I started to laugh. Human beings are really funny to look at . . . especially when naked. Let me correct this: I am funny to look at when naked.

Sometimes I catch myself being so serious . . . and I laugh.

I'm in such a hurry to go (really) nowhere . . . and I laugh.

I worry about things that are beyond my control . . . and I laugh.

Friends telephone and are stressed about other people, often trying to change them or get them to behave differently . . . and I laugh.

There is so much to laugh about.

Do you agree?

God created the world for fun.

God

Any God I ever felt in church I brought in with me. And I think all the other folks did, too. They come to church to share God, not find God.

—Alice Walker, The Color Purple

Say Yes to Your Spirit is more than just thinking about God. It is about experiencing, feeling the power of spirituality.

But what kind of a God do we believe in? For years I believed in an authoritarian God who judged good and bad actions, sending you to hell if you were very bad. Today I believe in Alice's God, a God who is discovered in people.

"Dancing in God" means that we all share in God's spiritual power; God's power is also discovered within each of us.

Namasté: the God in me recognizes and celebrates the God in you.

I reflect God in all that I do.

Change

There is nothing permanent except change.
—Heraclitus

For years I resisted change. I was probably a pessimist, preferring what I knew to what could be. Fear was the foundation for much of my life, and I forever feared what I did not know or understand.

Today I embrace change. Why? I changed. When I embraced recovery I not only did things differently but I also began to think differently. Change is the nature of life. Resisting change is still a part of change!

Say Yes to Your Spirit is becoming an optimist. I look forward to the future. When things are not working out for me I know that I can do things differently. Instead of kneeling before God, now I'm dancing in God; that in itself is a considerable change.

Today I live to change.

Humanity

To say that a man is made up of certain chemical elements is a satisfactory description only for those who intend to use him as a fertilizer.
—Hermann Joseph Muller

Say Yes to Your Spirit is daring to examine that part of every human being that cannot be seen, touched, or quantified; it is the soul of humanity. Yes, it is life, but it is also mysterious.

This concept is my spirituality today; it is the music between the notes, the poetry that is within every poet, and the vision that drives every artist. What is it? It is the *mysterium tremendum*: the creativity that fuels our dance in God.

Without this insight, life would be dull, basic, and animalistic. Unfortunately many people seem to live in this mode of existence.

Thank God I'm not one of them. You see, I still believe that we can fly.

After you have described and examined every inch of me, the mystery remains.

Prejudices

It is never too late to give up your prejudices.
—Henry David Thoreau

I used to be a prejudiced person. Today I know it was because I was fearful: fearful of change, fearful of difference, fearful of what I did not understand. I was fearful of anything that challenged my little world.

Then I got sober. I embraced recovery. My world suddenly became so much bigger, more exciting.

I danced with the foreigner, with the non-Christian, with the poor: I danced in God.

When I speak at meetings I often say that I am more than English, more than white, more than male, more than Christian. If you really want to know me, then come to the land of *More*!

When I begin to love,
I give up my prejudices.

Uniqueness

God sees nothing average.

—Author Unknown

I used to think that average was okay. It was acceptable to be ordinary. Being human was enough.

Then somebody suggested that I was unique. I said, "Okay."

"No, Leo. Listen to me. You are unique. There will never be another you. You are one of a kind."

"Okay," I replied.

"No, Leo. You are special, divine, and extraordinary."

Then I began to understand. If I think only within the boundary of "average," then that is all I will ever be. Once I realized I was divine, then creativity became an everyday tool. And my life forever is changing.

What about you?

Wherever I am, God is.

Originality

Originality does not consist in saying what no one has ever said before, but in saying exactly what you think yourself.
—James Stephens

Wow. I really needed to hear this. I was driving myself crazy trying to be original. All I needed to be was real.

Originality is being real: saying what I think, doing what I believe to be right, and occasionally confessing my confusion. I allow myself to change my mind.

If there are many paths to God, there are many paths to life. What's more, we can be on more than one path at the same time.

Originality is being honest. Being honest is being real. And this is divine.

What is truth?
It is being original.

Vision

Cherish your vision and your dreams as they are the children of your soul, the blueprints of your ultimate achievements.

—Napoleon Hill

My life would be nothing without vision. As I sit at my desk writing this affirmation, I'm seeing this book in print being read by people who are wanting to *Say Yes to Your Spirit.*

I also vision myself dancing in God. I have a joyous smile on my face because I know that if I remain positive and creative I can make my life better. I can also improve your life by my attitude.

I've said in this book that there is a poetic side to all of us . . . and poets dream dreams.

Today I can see what I want to be and where I want to go.

Values

A man who dares to waste one hour of time has not discovered the value of life.

—Charles Darwin

I think we all waste time, certainly more than one hour, and I'm sure this included Charles Darwin.

But he was writing to make us think. Darwin was practicing overstatement. His message: life is too valuable to waste.

Say Yes to Your Spirit envelops this message. Life is important. The way we speak about God and embrace people who are different is important. Living alongside differing opinions and ideas is important. To dance in God is to dance in difference.

All of the above are important: values make up the spiritual life.

Today I have values.
I also respect yours.

Dance

There are no mistakes in tango. It's like life.
If you get all tangled up, you tango on.
—Scent of a Woman (film)

I really liked this movie. The blind man dancing with the beautiful young woman, connected yet separate, made an important point about life: we are connected, yet separate.

When I dance in God I'm involved and also separate. It really is about emphasis: holding together more than one thought or idea, more than one truth.

My mother used to say that if you can dance, then you can understand life and other people. She is right. I also think that if you can dance, then you can understand God.

Say Yes to Your Spirit
with a dance.

Nature

According to accounts of Gautama Buddha's life, he had a deep relationship with nature. The Buddha was very fond of trees.
—Dalai Lama

I'm very pleased that the Buddha was fond of trees. I've read that the Dalai Lama is fond of trees. Personally, I'm very fond of cheese!

Nature is an important part of our *Say Yes to Your Spirit*. It feeds us, entertains us, inspires us. On a poetic level nature is who I am. Remember, Alice Walker wrote that if you cut the tree she bleeds.

Without nature there would be no life.

Nature is a friend with
a thousand faces.

Fear

Courage is resistance to fear, mastery of fear—not absence of fear.
—Mark Twain

Every morning that I attend a support meeting I hear something about fear. Rarely do I get through a day without experiencing fear. Fear seems an intimate part of life.

But where does it come from? It comes from anywhere and everywhere: parents, religion, law, society, school, church. Fear creates shame and guilt.

Say Yes to Your Spirit is about healing the fear. Notice I say "healing," not "removing" it. Each day brings new fears. But if we have a philosophy that is based upon love, then we can face our fears, heal our fears . . . maybe even dance with our fears.

I respect my fear.
But I respect my love much more.

Courage

Success is never final, and failure is never fatal.
It is courage that counts.
—Winston Churchill

Last night I watched a movie about Lawrence of Arabia. Some months ago I saw a movie about Gandhi. I've been inspired by biographies of François Fénelon, Golda Meir, and Mother Teresa. All had courage.

But so have we. We all have courage. Sometimes we discount ourselves by saying that our courage is nothing compared to "so and so"—but each step of courage is important:

- Affirming for the first time: *I'm an alcoholic.*
- Telling a friend, "That joke is not funny; it's racist."
- A wife calling a hotline and saying, "My husband is abusing me."
- One spouse informing the other, "I'm taking the children and leaving you."
- Admitting that God is not a prisoner of any religious law.

Wherever it is found, courage counts.

My Say Yes to Your Spirit *involves courage.*

Procrastination

Procrastination is opportunity's natural assassin.

—Victor Kiam

Some years ago I was a procrastinator. Why did I change? I realized I wasn't getting anywhere in my life.

- Tomorrow I'll stop drinking.
- In the morning I'll begin writing the book.
- Next week I'll apply for a job.
- I need to get a passport.
- This is the year I'll join a gym.

So it went on. And I was getting sicker, poorer, lonelier, fatter . . . and depressed. And then the pain created the change.

Today if something needs to happen I do it, *right away*, then I can forget about it. Action is creating success.

Today I will not postpone
my dance in God.

Effort

Work joyfully and peacefully, knowing that right thoughts and right efforts inevitably bring about right results.

—James Allen

This quotation affirms the importance of attitude in our deliberations and actions. Work is an essential part of *Say Yes to Your Spirit*. If you really intend to dance in God, then effort is required because we seek to change our world, on a daily basis, and make it loving and joyful.

Is that Pollyanna-ish? I don't think so. We are not trying to change the whole world; we are seeking to change *our* world . . . for the better.

- We greet the day with a smile.
- We have a positive affirmation for what we seek to accomplish.
- We are determined to treat all the people whom we meet with respect.

I will put God's effort into my day.

Imperfection

In the country of the blind, the one-eyed king can still goof up.

—Lawrence J. Peter

When I embraced Unity of Christianity I heard from my friends who are metaphysical, "We are perfect." Metaphysics promotes the idea that God is part of us and we are part of God . . . cocreation. "Instead of sin, think perfection." I really like this concept.

But I also know I carry a shadow. I can choose to be average. I can turn my back on God . . . diminishment. I don't like this aspect of my thinking and behavior, but I know it is there. Saying I'm divine does not stop me from also being human!

Friends say, "But human is divine." But not the human I'm living. The "goof-up" I live with is fear-based: insecure, envious, and dishonest.

Often I'm reaching for the stars with my feet in manure!

Today I can goof up,
then move on.

Habits

Motivation is what gets you started. Habit is what keeps you going.

—Jim Ryun

In most meditation books, you don't often read about "habits." Yet when you begin to think about it, habits are important. Don't confuse habits with hobbies!

I know I don't really have a hobby, unless you include fine dining, travel, and going to the cinema. I don't play golf, tennis, or soccer or ride a mountain bike on weekends. But I have some good habits:

- I sit at my desk and write even when I don't feel like writing.
- I clean up the kitchen as I go along. That way it doesn't get out of control and become a gigantic mess at the end of the day.
- I discipline myself to read one book at a time.
- I go to bed early and try to wake up early.
- I place the things I need for the morning at my front door the previous night.

My habits help me create a positive and creative life.

Beauty

Everything has its beauty, but not everyone sees it.
—Confucius

An alcoholic priest wakes up in a treatment center. He looks out of the window and sees the sun rising. He asks, "How long has that been happening?"

I didn't see the forest for the trees. Beauty was under my nose all the time. When I *Say Yes to Your Spirit*, I appreciate nature: I'm cognizant of what is happening on a daily basis in my world:

- The birds singing.
- The creativity of the weather.
- The loving people around me.
- The wonderment of technology.
- The gratitude for my daily bread.

Beauty is not only in faces or the opposite sex or so-called masterpieces. Beauty is life.

I'm dancing with my eyes open.

Determination

For the resolute and determined there is time and opportunity.
—Ralph Waldo Emerson

I don't have to do everything today. I always have tomorrow. I want to work smarter, not harder.

It's taken me a long time to realize this, and it is part of my recovery. For too many years I chased success, that is, love and God. Then, a few years back, I began to relax. I had time. And I realized that life is time, an accumulation of minutes.

Don't misunderstand me. I'm still resolute and determined, but today I give myself some space. I'm not responsible for the world, only my life.

I'm taking the day off.

I don't need to dance every dance!

Honesty

Honesty is the first chapter in the book of wisdom.
—Thomas Jefferson

Say Yes to Your Spirit is about honesty. Spirituality is about honesty. The Golden Rule requires honesty. Honesty is the basis of all the great religions, and no leader who proclaims righteousness can exist without it.

- Honesty enables a person to be real.
- Honesty allows a person to be known.
- Honesty helps determine right actions.
- Honesty creates humility.

When I was drinking I was dishonest because I was ashamed. I'm always dishonest when I'm trying to hide. Today I'm slowly moving out of the shadows. Honesty has become my vehicle.

I want to dance in God, but I also want to dance in the light.

Fun

From there to here, and here to there, funny things are everywhere.
—Dr. Seuss

When we *Say Yes to Your Spirit* we are aware that life can be funny, humorous, and sometimes even hilarious.

There was a time in my life when I was too, too serious. The religion of my childhood played a role in keeping me serious; God was judgmental, angry, and *all-seeing*. I was often seized by fear when I entered a church.

Today my God is loving, less serious. Now, please don't misunderstand me. I really need to be responsible in my life, but I can be responsible with a smile on my face.

The thought of every day waking to dance in God keeps me smiling.

Fun is an essential part of the spiritual life.

Goodness

Neither fire nor wind, birth nor death can erase our good deeds.
—Gautama Buddha

I remember saying recently at a support meeting that I wanted to be a good person. Not "perfect," "good."

Seeking to live *Say Yes to Your Spirit* is about *goodness* . . . seeing the best in ourselves and others.

Each day gives us an opportunity to practice our goodness:

- Call a friend and say hello.
- Smile at a neighbor across the street.
- Forgive ourselves for an indiscretion.
- Send money to a charity in need.

When we practice goodness, we feel better about life.

It is in our own interest to do good things, because then good things return to us: a spiritual karma.

I want to do good things in life because it is a good way to live.

Wisdom

Forget injuries. Never forget kindnesses.
—Confucius

I heard a therapist say that when we forgive we are not expected to forget. And I really understood what he was saying; some things are too hard to forget or should never be forgotten.

But wisdom has many sides. Sometimes we are able to forget—not only forgive, but actually forget. It is as if a word or action never happened.

When we dance in God we forget everything else and enjoy the moment: free, sacred, spontaneous.

Thank you, God, for the gift of spiritual forgetfulness.

Ingenuity

Success is the maximum utilization of the ability that you have.
—Zig Ziglar

The word "ingenuity" is not used frequently in connection with spirituality, but it is so apposite. "Apposite" is another word that is rarely used.

When we *Say Yes to Your Spirit* we create from the many parts of us that make us human, and in this way we become successful.

Religion is not the only path to God. Indeed, for many people religion has not been helpful. Still, they have found a way to understanding God through poetry, art, music . . . sometimes suffering.

When we are dancing in God we can use any steps that we find helpful.

Today I am polishing the
gift of ingenuity.

Honor

Rather fail with honor than succeed by fraud.

—Sophocles

I don't think you can live *Say Yes to Your Spirit* without being concerned for personal honor.

What is honor? Well, it's not about being perfect, but it is about wanting to be good. Notice I say "wanting to be good"; you might not be there yet.

Some of us have challenges that make the spiritual life difficult: alcoholism, addiction, depression, schizophrenia, and so on. We may need treatment or medication before we can begin the journey to personal honor.

Being honorable does not necessarily mean that you are religious, but it does involve spirituality.

The days that I allow myself to dance in God are the days that I'm close to being honorable.

Today I connect honor
with being real.

Opportunity

In the middle of difficulty lies opportunity.
—Albert Einstein

Wow. I needed to hear this sentence. Thank you, Albert.

This is one of those days when I'm surrounded by difficulties, challenges, and misunderstandings . . . all caused by me. Sometimes I really am my biggest enemy.

What to do? I face them. Take it one hour at a time. Keep putting one foot in front of the other. Learn from the challenges I face.

That is often my problem, I don't learn from my challenges, and so I'm doomed to repeat my mistakes.

Being human is never easy. But what is the alternative? I must surrender, change, and do things differently.

Today I'm really ready to
Say Yes to Your Spirit.

July

Creativity

I've always been in the right place at the right time. Of course, I steered myself there.
—Bob Hope

Occasionally I feel at odds with what is happening in my life. I'm not in a good place, or my daily serenity is absent.

Having a bad day is okay. Maybe it's not too late to change it. But if it is too late there is always tomorrow. That is part of *Say Yes to Your Spirit*: we can creatively change.

You may be facing some serious challenges today, and if you really don't know what to do, then don't do anything. Often, if you wait until tomorrow or discuss the challenge with a trusted friend, a solution will appear.

Don't beat yourself up. That is not going to help and will only make matters worse.

I'm sad today. But I imagine myself dancing tomorrow.

Character

The chief factor in any man's success or failure must be his own character.

—Theodore Roosevelt

What is character? I don't think it is something that is formed in isolation; rather it is a compilation of all the people whom we read about or meet. The challenges that we face in life all come together to enhance our character or diminish it.

Today I'm very much aware of the shadows in my life that make me realize there are certain things I need to do if I am to maintain any semblance of success. *Say Yes to Your Spirit* is knowing that I grow my character. I am responsible not only for my outer appearance but also for my interior self.

I know I'm dancing in God, but today I'm a little slower.

I am responsible for developing good character.

Heroism

He whom prosperity humbles, and adversity strengthens, is the true hero.
—Josh Billings

I watched a biography concerning the life of the Reverend Martin Luther King Jr. I knew that he had faced great adversity, but when I saw the opposition, prejudice, and violence he endured, I became a greater admirer of what he had achieved.

I've had adversity in my life. Today I understand that it is how I respond to it that truly makes the difference as to how I overcome it. *Say Yes to Your Spirit* involves my response to adversity because I'm not going to get through life without experiencing it.

And I'm helped by others, especially by a program that talks about what it was like, what happened, and what it is like now. It is from the "what happened" and my response to it that my personal heroism emerges.

Today I want to be my own hero.

Patriotism

Patriotism . . . applies to true love of one's country and a code of conduct that echoes such love.
—Howard Fast

I was born in England, and I love to read about the history of my country. I especially enjoy reading about Sir Winston Churchill and the many speeches that he made. He was a true patriot.

Some years ago I became a citizen of the United States. I'm proud to be an American, and today I'm reading about this country and the famous men and women who have contributed to its charter of liberty.

Liberty is not only an idea; it is also a code of behavior. If I am to enjoy freedom, then I need to encourage the experience of freedom in others—and not just my fellow citizens.

In my Say Yes to Your Spirit, *I realize I'm a patriot of the world.*

Old Age

In youth we learn. In old age we understand.
—Marie von Ebner-Eschenbach

How true that saying is for me.

When I was a young man I went to school to learn about God, history, geography, and the arts. I learned about names, dates, and philosophical concepts, but only as I've aged have I begun to understand them.

My *Say Yes to Your Spirit* is about understanding that there are many paths to God, and not all of them are religious.

I understand that wars rarely create peace; peace can only come when people respect and accept each other's differences.

I also understand that heroes, famous men and women of history, could only create their achievements with the support of ordinary men and women whose names we will never know.

Today I know less and understand more.

Judgment

Why do you look at the speck of sawdust in your brother's eye and pay no attention to the plank in your own eye?

—Jesus (Matthew 7:3)

It is so easy to judge other people. I've been working on that character defect for years. However, when I get angry in my judgments of others it is usually because *something* is too close to home.

I've been doing some serious work on myself lately. I'm especially attentive to examining my personal character defects. I write about them and see them for what they are—in a word, "insecurity." Slowly I'm beginning to heal.

I'm also discovering as I do this work on myself that I'm less judgmental toward others.

And I'm a happier person.

I believe that only when I can remove the specks that are in my own eye will I be able to love you.

Anger

Anger is never without a reason, but seldom with a good one.
—Benjamin Franklin

I used to be so angry. Today I realize that my anger was fed by my personal insecurities that in turn were fed by my alcoholism.

I needed a reason to be angry. If I didn't have one, then I would manufacture one. It was a sad life.

Today I rarely get angry. Why? Because I seek to live *Say Yes to Your Spirit.*

- In the morning, I read an affirmation book.
- I attend a support group.
- I'm discovering God in nature.
- I'm truly aware of those parts of me that require healing.

All the above help me accept others.
And I'm less angry.

My anger is my responsibility.
Occasionally it is appropriate anger.

Natural

Some beautiful things are more impressive when left imperfect than when too highly finished.
—François de La Rochefoucauld

I read somewhere that human beings are angels in the dirt. I like that.

Sometimes our imperfections and failings are what make us loveable. I think it could be the grit that produces the pearl.

Say Yes to Your Spirit is about how we face our challenges in life and become better, more spiritual people. Could we ever become spiritual without those challenges? That is an interesting question, but a question that is moot because we all have challenges, failings, and issues to face in our lives. I'm an alcoholic. It has opened the door to an understanding of spirituality that has taken me beyond religion, beyond denominationalism—and I'm a better person because of it.

My dance in God is imperfect, but real.

Understanding

I hear and I forget. I see and I remember.
I do and I understand.
—Confucius

All of the sayings in this book force us to think. Ideally, after thinking comes the action. Confucius seems to be saying that only when we get into action will we understand. I've found this to be true.

- When I seek to show love, only then do I begin to understand it.
- When I share my recovery with others, I'm able to understand what it is.
- When I forgive, I'm able to get a glimpse into forgiveness.
- When I talk about my shame, I'm able to understand where it comes from.

Action leads to understanding.

Only when I walk my talk do
I understand my message.

Leadership

A leader is best when people barely know he exists, when his work is done, his aim fulfilled, they will say: we did it ourselves.
—Lao-tzu

I suppose I'm like many people who for years thought that leadership was being "out front"—taking the responsibility but also taking the praise.

But there is a different kind of leadership, what I like to call "quiet leadership," that nurtures a person or group from the sidelines.

- The sponsor who speaks in the evening to many people, and yet his work is always anonymous.
- The wise parent who suggests to his or her child, from personal experience, how to negotiate life.
- The manager of an office who establishes firm boundaries so that each employee is responsible for his or her assignments.

Say Yes to Your Spirit often establishes this "great leadership" that affirms personal responsibility.

Today I'm able to lead from behind.

Humility

Never underestimate your power to change yourself; never overestimate your power to change others.

—H. Jackson Brown Jr.

In my early Christian years I thought that humility was about sacrificing myself to the needs of others, in some cases allowing them to take advantage of me. Then I discovered that the root meaning of the word "humility" is being of the earth . . . no better than another person but also no worse.

Humility breeds a gentle confidence that always affords respect.

With this new understanding of humility I'm able to slowly work on myself and, in the words of the Serenity Prayer, "change the things I can." I also understand that there are many things I cannot change, and that includes you!

Say Yes to Your Spirit affirms that I'm responsible for changing me. With advice and nurture, you are responsible for changing yourself.

Today I'm able to give you space
to create your own dance.

Imitation

Children have never been very good at listening to their elders, but they have never failed to imitate them.

—James Baldwin

Imitation is the highest form of flattery.

When we embrace *Say Yes to Your Spirit* we realize that many people influence our lives, often without realizing it. Even crazy behavior has an influence because it teaches us what not to do!

I never realized how much my mother has influenced my life until she died some years ago. I remember her words in the kitchen over tea: "You get what you create."

But more than what she said, I remember how she behaved with other people. The encouraging smile, her silences that allowed me to find my words, the way she kept her space in life neat and tidy.

I catch myself imitating her behavior, and I smile.

My life has been a shared experience.

Intuition

Intuition is perception via the unconscious.
—Carl Jung

Say Yes to Your Spirit is obviously concerned with spirituality. For years I've always wanted to include in the concept of spirituality the body, mind, and emotions.

How we treat our bodies, what we eat, and getting adequate rest are important.

Feeding our mind with positive thoughts and stories helps us to continue with an intention of optimism.

Our feelings—being able to express appropriately our love, fear, and anger—are all part of living the "spiritual awakening."

But then there is the unconscious. That part of ourselves is difficult to describe and yet is the seed of our natural and God-given intuition. How is this nurtured? By taking care of all the above and surrounding ourselves with people who are doing the same.

Jesus said it: "Having eyes do you not see?" Our job is to keep our eyes clear.

Today I'm guided by my intuition.

Peace

Peace comes from within. Do not seek it without.
—Gautama Buddha

There have been times in my life when I've felt so ashamed about what I have said or done: times when I didn't like myself . . . and I'm not at peace.

What can I do when I feel like this? Well, I feel the feelings. I look at what I am doing that needs radical change. And I try to stay in the now—living one day at a time.

St. John of the Cross called it "the dark night of the soul." It eventually passes; the day follows the night. It's life, and it's part of the spiritual life. Everyone has such times, but my experience teaches me that such times eventually pass. Then, yes, we're able to dance again.

I'm doing all that I can to maintain peace in my life.

Life

Life is 10 percent what happens to me and 90 percent how I react to it.
—Lou Holtz

I needed to read this today. Things are not going exactly the way I wish: problems at work, misunderstandings, decisions that require a radical change in the way I'm living my life. I'm having an uncomfortable day.

What must I do? Well, I know that I should not overreact. Yes, there are some things that I need to do, but more than anything I should spend time with my feelings: rest, feel, and then develop a sensible plan for my life.

Say Yes to Your Spirit is about developing a healthy balance in my life, and today I'm having a wake-up call. But I'm not going to overreact.

I've learned in my life not only to count sheep but also that I can count to ten.

Diversity

Diversity is both beautiful and necessary.

—Dalai Lama

Yesterday I was not feeling on top of the world, but today I'm feeling really good. How do we change? It's not how one day can be so different from another (actually I'm not sure it's the days that change, although the weather always affects my mood), but rather how we react to change.

Diversity is really about the variety and changes that are in creation, in human beings, in life itself.

We all dance differently because we *are* different, which makes for the beauty in creation.

Say Yes to Your Spirit is the acceptance of this diversity, rather than denying it or fighting it. God has made each of us delightfully different.

Today I'm able to appreciate and grow in the precious gift of diversity.

Management

The ultimate test of management is performance.
—Peter F. Drucker

I suppose when you make the decision to dance in God there is choreography, steps that need to be decided upon, and a certain style that leads to a better performance.

Many people would consider it too much of a stretch to connect management with spirituality, but is it? Throughout this book we encounter the word "responsibility," the ability to respond to life, which requires a certain management of our lives.

Life teaches us that there are some things we can do and some things we should not do. Some behaviors are acceptable, and some, if left untreated, can destroy our lives.

When I *Say Yes to Your Spirit* I affirm that I need to manage my life in a Godly direction.

I seek to manage my life
in a spiritual manner.

Future

The future belongs to those who believe in the beauty of their dreams.
—Eleanor Roosevelt

I've often been told not to live in the future, better to stay in the now. And I agree.

We all, however, have dreams for what our life could be like. John Lennon said it for the world when he sang,

> You may say I'm a dreamer.
> But I'm not the only one.

I have a dream for a better tomorrow. Not just for me, but for everyone. Yes, I'm an optimist. But I don't think that my life or anyone else's is necessarily going to be perfect . . . just better.

Essentially *Say Yes to Your Spirit* is about being an optimist, dreaming dreams for change so that all people can be free of their demons, their shackles. Why not? If enough of us embrace *Say Yes to Your Spirit*, then the energy in the universe might indeed change for the better.

I believe in a better tomorrow.

Kindness

Forget injuries, never forget kindnesses.
—Confucius

I suppose another word for this meditation could be "gratitude." Kindness and gratitude are connected because we are usually grateful for the kindnesses that we receive in our lives.

This connection certainly holds for me. Sometimes I include in my morning meditation a reflection on those who have showed me kindness . . . and they are legion. Here are just a few:

- My parents.
- Friends.
- The recovering community.
- The people with whom I'm fortunate enough to work.
- Writers in history who have influenced my life.
- Singers I've never met but who brighten up my days.
- My pets.

It might be a good idea to spend some moments thinking about the kindnesses you have received in your life.

I show kindness because I need kindness.

Self-Esteem

Trust yourself. You know more than you think.

—Benjamin Spock

Do I trust myself? Sometimes.

The days that I do not trust my judgment, when I'm insecure, are when I am off beam: I'm too tired, I've not eaten, I'm stressed, or I'm in a bad mood. Winston Churchill used to call these times "the day of the black dog."

Fortunately, they are not too often. Why? Well, I'm taking better care of myself.

- I go to bed early.
- I eat sensibly.
- I stay around positive people.

Because of these simple life exercises I find I'm in a better mood, more optimistic, happier. And my self-esteem has improved.

Then I'm able to trust myself, and I realize what Dr. Benjamin Spock has said: I really do know more than I think I do.

My Say Yes to Your Spirit
involves trusting myself.

Performance

An ant on the move does more than a dozing ox.

—Lao-tzu

One step at a time; don't rush, but keep moving forward. Success is a process.

I need to remember that today. I wish to work smarter, not harder. For too many years I rushed around like a chicken with its head cut off—activity rather than performance.

Say Yes to Your Spirit is more cautionary. I need to think before I act, and I don't need to rush.

Today I have a work plan. I write down three or four things that I want to achieve each day. When I'm done I find time to play. I don't waste time; rather I seek to create my life on a daily basis.

It works for me. What about you?

Fools rush in . . . not me!

Pacifism

Using violence is against human nature.
The concept of war is out of date.
—Dalai Lama

The world does not seem to have heard what the Dalai Lama has said; war and aggression seem to be all over the place.

But maybe not. It often appears as if the world is in a state of chaos because the news media responds instantly and endlessly, and bad news sells. However, I believe that the world is less violent, less aggressive, and less hostile than in the past. More people are choosing diplomacy over war, and democracy is growing in many parts of the world.

- Women are more liberated.
- Overt prejudice is outlawed.
- Cultural respect is growing.

The world is becoming a better place to live for more and more people.

Is there more to do? Absolutely! That is the message of *Say Yes to Your Spirit.*

Today I envision a world moving toward peace.

Memories

History is the seedbed of the future.

—Leo Booth

I have a lot of memories—some good, some not so good. But I learn from them.

In my recovery story I talk about the moment when I saw myself after a drunken car accident. It was the moment that led me into recovery.

But real recovery is not based upon a single moment; it is about keeping that moment alive and embracing more moments. These special moments that lead to change are based upon memories.

Thank God that I can remember. It is often painful, and yet in a mysterious way miraculous. With remembrance comes change.

If I want a better tomorrow,
I must be prepared to remember the past.

Obesity

Obesity is really widespread.

—Joseph O. Kern II

A funny remark! And true.

Say Yes to Your Spirit requires that we look at obesity. If people need healing from alcoholism, drug addiction, gambling, and workaholism, then we cannot neglect compulsive eating.

I was told that overeating is a primary addiction, meaning that from being little babies, if we cried we were given milk or food. Pain followed by food!

Most of us move away from food and embrace alcohol, cigarettes, drugs, or sex, but some people spend their lives dealing with food issues. The answer is spiritual: to know that we have the personal power, in cooperation with God, to change our lives. Thousands of people are doing just that on a daily basis. It has been said, "It's not what you are eating; it's what's eating you!" When we are prepared to look at the pain in our lives, we will also discover the healing.

Today I'm developing a food plan in my life.

Religion

It is the test of a good religion if you can joke about it.

—G. K. Chesterton

When it comes to my religion I can joke about it.

- I saw a sign on the freeway that said, "Don't let worry kill you. Let the church help!"
- This morning's sermon will be "Jesus walks on the water." And this evening's sermon, "Searching for Jesus."
- The church is starting a support group for people with low self-esteem. Please use the back door!

I also think that God had a sense of humor when God created us. If you don't believe me, take off all your clothes and look in the mirror.

Today my God is smiling when
we dance in life together.

Faith

Faith is never identical with piety.

—Karl Barth

When I was very religious I would genuflect in church, make the sign of the cross, rattle my rosary beads, and murmur prayers so that everybody knew I was praying. I had piety but little faith.

Today I'm more spiritual. I have faith not only in my understanding of God but also your understanding of God. *Namasté*! I not only believe that Christianity is a path to God, but I also believe that there are other paths to God, religious and nonreligious. This is my understanding of *Say Yes to Your Spirit.*

Also I have a faith in myself today. There is a divinity within me that allows me to love and heal others and myself.

I have joy today. Now can you understand why I am dancing in God?

I do not want to be a hypocrite
in God's world.

Belief

An atheist is a man who has no invisible means of support.
—Anonymous

Some days my belief in God is sure, clear, and definite. Other times I'm not so sure. I truly understand the human cry, "Lord, I believe. Help thou my unbelief."

But I've never really been an atheist. The world seems too amazing—and that's before we consider the universe! I'm also amazed at humankind, at myself. What human beings are able to achieve through science, music, art, philosophy, literature, adventure, medicine, politics . . . the list could go on and on. We are even able to reflect upon the "dark side" of human nature, on ourselves, and slowly begin the healing process.

Sometimes I find myself feeling agnostic because I don't understand the mystery. Then I remember that mystery is not meant to be understood.

I believe in a power greater than myself.

Saints

Every saint has a past and every sinner a future.
—Oscar Wilde

Wearing my religious hat for the moment, I know that religious people can be very judgmental. You might respond by saying that people can be judgmental. True. But aren't religious people supposed to be forgiving, accepting, and understanding?

I believe there are arguments to be made on all sides, but proponents of any dogmatic or rigid religion, especially concerning an interpretation of the Bible, usually live to regret their rigidity.

- Saints are usually sinners who have changed their clothes.
- Sinners always have a chance to change their clothes.
- A saint is a holy person. And a holy person, in my eyes, is forever forgiving.

Why? Because they remember their past.

Today I'm content to be the best human being that I can be.

Flexibility

Better bend than break.

—Scottish Proverb

Kevin Taylor is a friend of mine who always says, "We need to be flexible. We are all free to change our minds." He is right.

In society, religion, or politics, if we become too rigid, too dogmatic, or too sure of ourselves, we live to regret it.

Have we forgotten that word, "change"? It is intimately connected with flexibility. Flexibility and change form the foundation of *Say Yes to Your Spirit*.

We know from experience that all rules will at times be broken, and we need to be flexible in our response to the offender. We live in a world that emanates diversity by its very nature. We suffer if we are not flexible in our response to this world.

Today I'm seeking to be
a flexible dancer.

Unity

This land of ours cannot be a good place to live in unless we make it a good place for all of us to live in.

—Richard Nixon

I was surprised when I read that Richard Nixon had said these words. But remembering yesterday's reading, perhaps I should be flexible in my assessment of any human being. We are all complex characters.

Also I'm reminded that "unity" is not the same word as "uniformity." We can be connected without all being the same.

Say Yes to Your Spirit is knowing that God speaks through many cultures, languages, and creeds; no one path is the only path to understanding God.

I'm content to be a student in life, which means that I must find a comfortable place for me to learn. If I'm to learn from you, I need to ensure that you are comfortable.

I understand that unity is God's prayer for creation.

Conscience

In matters of conscience, the law of the majority has no place.
—Mahatma Gandhi

The majority is not right just because it is the majority. Some terrible things have happened in history that were supported by the majority of people. Examples include slavery, racism, sexism, and homophobia.

We all need to go to that interior part of ourselves and ask these questions:

- What do I believe?
- How do I live alongside people who are different?
- Am I willing to stand alone for the things that I believe?

We all know that to follow our conscience requires inner strength and conviction. Few will succeed every time, which is why we all need the gift of forgiveness.

Today I try to follow my conscience.

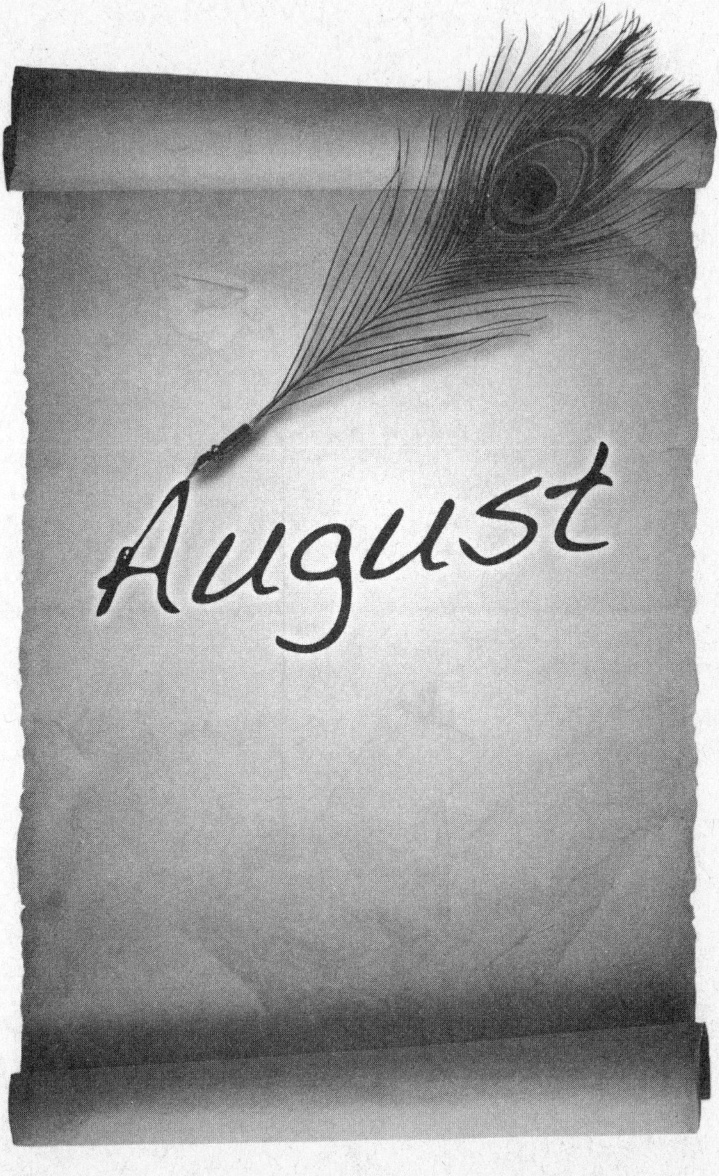
August

Being

For forty years I've been selling water. By the bank of a river. Ho, Ho! My labors have been wholly without merit.

—Sogaku Harada

This seems a funny saying, but maybe not. Maybe it is okay not to be always seeking to achieve something.

The psalmist said, "Be still and know that I am God." Just be still . . . and know.

When we *Say Yes to Your Spirit*, we determine to look at many aspects of life—and then we rest. It is okay to be still, not doing anything in particular.

Sometimes when I go to the zoo I look at the animals, and they mostly seem content not to be doing anything. They sit around under the trees or just stare at nothing. They are happy just to be.

When I toured Vietnam I visited a monastery, and the head monk guided me around. We went into a room with twenty monks just sitting on carpets.

"Are they praying?" I asked.

"No, they are practicing just being. It's enough."

To be is enough.

Work

I have nothing to offer but blood, toil, tears, and sweat.

—Winston Churchill

Work is a gift from God. We can make a better life for ourselves and the people whom we love.

But sometimes, especially in times of war and conflict, we need to work very hard to survive. Not everything will go the way we want in life, and sacrifice is often an aspect of work.

Winston Churchill understood this. Martin Luther King Jr. knew this to be true. Mother Teresa spoke about this in her work with the poor.

Say Yes to Your Spirit takes this concept very seriously because we all know that our world is separated and divided with conflicts on every continent. But with work we can overcome the difficulties and bring about peace and security.

I'm willing to work for this belief.

Thank you, God,
for making me creative.

Service

Living beings are numberless; I vow to serve until all are liberated.

—Vows to the Bodhisattvas

I heard at a recovery meeting this morning that the key to sobriety lies in the service of others; when I am willing to give my recovery away, then I get to keep it.

Say Yes to Your Spirit involves service: being available to other people, realizing that the world does not revolve simply around me. Other people are involved.

It was good for me to hear this message this morning. I grapple with being self-centered, selfish, and ego-focused, and I don't always make myself available to others. When I do make myself available, though, I feel so good, useful, purposeful, and satisfied.

I know that I need to take care of me, but I should never forget the needs of others. I've observed that when I enter the discipleship of service, I receive in abundance.

I maintain my liberty when
I enter into service.

Citizenship

I am not an Athenian or a Greek, but a citizen of the world.
—Socrates

I really like the idea of being a citizen of the world. I was born in England and I'm a documented citizen of the United States, but my understanding of spirituality teaches me that I'm connected to the world, not simply a country.

Throughout this book I've said that religion and spirituality are not the same. For me, spirituality is like a golden thread that connects all the religions, making a world religion. But more than religion, I believe that all the great and noble ideas that can be found in poetry, art, and philosophy are also included. Once we are able to break down the borders that separate us, only then are we able to connect with other people and other religions.

This is the goal of *Say Yes to Your Spirit.*

Today I know I am a
citizen of the world.

Contemplation

Man is the matter of the cosmos, contemplating itself.

—Carl Sagan

Today I know that I am part of the cosmos. I know that I belong to something that is so much greater than I am, and yet, because I am a part of it, I share in its greatness.

This is why it is important to stress that *Say Yes to Your Spirit* is so much bigger and more inclusive than religion. Nothing is excluded; even the pain, suffering, and natural disasters that surround us are mysteriously involved. This is why we need the poets, philosophers, scientists, and yes, the cynics.

When John Donne told us that no person is an island, he was not just thinking about people, but the cosmos. And when we are able to take time to contemplate the cosmos, we are contemplating ourselves.

When I dance for joy in the forest,
God is involved.

Poetry

Our poetry now is the realization that we possess nothing. Anything therefore is a delight, since we do not possess it, and thus need not fear its loss.
—John Gage

I really love poetry. Why? Because it makes us think in a way that regular prose does not make us think.

We all know that at some level we can never fully understand or describe God. We also know, because God is a mystery, that it is equally difficult to describe our relationship with God or God's relationship to us.

Poetry helps us live with this mystery. It is able to bring together ideas that normally would not live alongside each other . . . and the paradox makes sense.

John Gage is suggesting that when we know that we do not really possess anything, we should not fear losing it—and this includes knowledge.

When I know that I do not know, then I am free.

Purity

From the outset your own nature is pure.

—The P'u-sa-chieh

I wonder if you were raised like me, to believe that I was born in sin: not exactly bad, but definitely "fallen." I could never really understand why. I still can't, but I had to accept it if I was to be a good Christian. Original sin, the inherited stain from Adam and Eve!

I don't believe that anymore. That's why I really like the quotation for this day. *Say Yes to Your Spirit* is always trying to affirm the positive. We are divine children from a Divine Creator who loves us and wants us to love.

This approach makes more sense to me. When I look at a newborn baby I see a wonderful purity that nurtures my optimism in the unlimited possibilities of human beings.

Yes, the world can mess all of us up in different ways, but I still believe that we are essentially good, which is why I am dancing in God.

I celebrate and seek to nurture my God-given purity.

Responsibility

Let him who would move the world first move himself.
—Socrates

I find it helpful to have a plan concerning what I want to do on any given day. I write notes to myself in the evening for what I want to achieve the following day.

- Pay any outstanding bills.
- Telephone friends.
- Begin making notes on articles I need to write.
- Go to the bank.
- Clean the guest bedroom.

Say Yes to Your Spirit is really about being responsible for my life. We all have things that need to be done. If we leave them for too long, we experience stress. My dance in God involves being responsible for everyday things, and when they are completed, I can relax.

I joyously embrace the gift of being responsible.

Poverty

The frustration of poverty leads to anger, then violence, violence among children. You can't blame individual people. The whole society is at fault.

—Mother Teresa

I was not born poor. I've never involuntarily gone a day without food. Each day I sleep in a sheltered environment.

But this is not true for many people. Poverty is, some would say, the biggest challenge facing our world. It breeds violence, anger, and exploitation.

What can we do about it? Well, it is important to know about it, to know that many people are suffering and that their suffering will, at times, affect us. Pray about it? Sure, but we need to do more than say prayers; we need to involve ourselves in the many projects that are created to feed the poor and empower the victims. At the very least we should contribute money.

But I'm just one person? One person who shares her or his commitment can change the world.

I begin my prayer with a written check.

Change

People can change. Make the effort, take the time, and change yourself.

—Leo Booth

Say Yes to Your Spirit is the belief that people can change themselves and the world in which they live.

Isn't that God's job? I used to think so, but I don't anymore. I believe that we all share in God's divinity and that we, at any time, can begin to create miracles.

What about prayer? Yes, we all need to pray, but we must also move our feet. This is the power of cocreation. This is what it means to dance in God.

- Alcoholics are embracing recovery.
- The uneducated are going back to school.
- The victims of violence are learning to empower themselves.
- Minorities are speaking up.

People can change. You can change. I have changed. Are you ready?

When I dance in God,
I'm initiating change.

Experience

I embrace energizing experience. I participate in discovery. I am a butterfly. I am not a butterfly collector.

—William Stafford

When I was a young man, I had a chance to leave home and go to the university, but I was scared. My mother took me into the kitchen. The kitchen was her study. Over a cup of tea, she said, "This will be a good experience for you. If it doesn't work out, you can always come home." Experience!

I had a chance to leave England and come to America. I told my parents. Again I was afraid. We went into the kitchen, another cup of tea. "This will be a good experience for you. If it doesn't work out, you can always come home."

Experience! It involves taking risks. It's always about change. It usually is successful if nurtured in love.

You are a butterfly. Surround yourself with love.

Today I understand that love enables the experience.

Karma

Which do you think is larger, the highest mountain on earth or the pile of bones that represent the lives that you have lived over and over in every realm governed by the patterns of your own karma? Greater, my friends, is the pile of bones than the highest mountain on earth.

—Gautama Buddha

I was not raised with the idea of reincarnation. One life seemed enough . . . more than enough.

Then I began to meet people who spoke about feeling that they had experienced other lives. They keep returning to learn the lessons they had not learned in their previous lives. I've occasionally had the feeling that I had been in a certain place or country before; it's a strange feeling.

Do I believe it? I don't really know. But it makes a certain kind of sense: the way we live not only determines the karma but also the life of the spiritual lessons.

Today I'm open to different spiritual solutions.

Peace

Peace will not come from the sky.

—Rev. Martin Luther King Jr.

It seems clear to me that we needed to do more than hope that the Nazis would go away.

Martin Luther King Jr. knew that people needed to do more than pray about racial integration.

Sometimes we need to put our body where our mouth has been for years!

Winston Churchill once said that an appeaser believes that if he feeds the tiger, the tiger will eat him last!

Say Yes to Your Spirit is about our willingness to confront violence, racism, sexism, and prejudice to create a more harmonious world. We will all confront it differently, but confront it we must. We all have our special dance and each person's steps will be different, but the movement will miraculously become ONE.

Peace is an intention that needs to be demonstrated.

Nature

Although we do not believe that trees or flowers have minds, we treat them also with respect. Thus we share a sense of universal responsibility for both mankind and nature.

—Lao-tzu

Spirituality involves nature. It is not enough to care for people if we do not care for the planet.

How do I care for the Earth that nurtures and feeds me?

- I pick up any trash that I see on the street.
- I recycle.
- I show respect to all animals, especially wild animals that require their space.
- I feed my plants and water my garden.
- When I speak about God and spirituality, I always include nature.
- I support nature charities.

When I care for my body, I am the beneficiary. So it is with nature. When I take care of the planet, I am the beneficiary.

I am blessed to have Brother Sun and Brother Wolf in my life.

Intelligence

Man must not forget to use his special gift of intelligence to triumph over conflict and disharmony.

—Albert Einstein

At a support group a friend told me that his sponsor had said, "Don't think. You think too much. You need to get out of your way, forget *your* plans. . . . Only then will God's plan be made manifest." I understand this advice. For some people it can be helpful.

But it really is a matter of emphasis. Are we really suggesting that a person with a problem—alcohol, drugs, whatever—doesn't think about it?

Say Yes to Your Spirit celebrates the power of intelligence in every human being. We need to speak and listen, affirm and be guided.

Many of the problems that human beings have had to face, and are facing, can only be overcome by a collective intelligence . . . a celebration of our divinity.

Today I know I have a brain, and I will use it in overcoming my problems.

Wisdom

The only true wisdom is in knowing you know nothing.
—Socrates

This is an exaggerated statement. There are many things that I do know: my age, my parents, where I was born, and where I live. However, many things I do not know, usually pertaining to God and spirituality.

- Why is there suffering in the world?
- What happens to us when we die?
- What does the future hold for me?
- What are animals thinking about?

This fact—that there is so much that we do not know or understand—allows for discussion, sharing of ideas, philosophy. This awareness allows me to be flexible and considerate to those who hold different opinions than my own.

Today I can accept that there are many things I do not know.

Creativity

Each man's future is in his own hands.

—Author Unknown

Some years ago I settled upon a definition of spirituality that involved two words: positive and creative. Religion is different from spirituality, involving an emphasis on denominationalism, creeds, and beliefs. With this comes a certain language. But spirituality is more inclusive, less defined, and needing its own language. Being positive and creative seemed to fit the bill for me.

Say Yes to Your Spirit continues this spiritual theme and emphasizes personal responsibility.

- What changes do you need to make in your life?
- What are you prepared to let go?
- Do you understand that prayer and worship require an understanding of partnership with God?

In a real and spiritual way we create our futures.

I am ready to make my
prayers come true.

Connection

How often have you been willing to look at your face in the mirror, without being embarrassed? That is the sixty-four-thousand-dollar question: how much have you connected with yourself and all in your whole life?

—Sogaku Harada

Say Yes to Your Spirit is really about connection; making a connection with God, with nature, with other people, and with ourselves.

For many years I used to wash my face, comb my hair, and get away from the mirror as quickly as possible. I was embarrassed at grooming myself: taking time to look at my eyebrows, chin, ears, and face. Why? Because I was raised to think that it was vanity. And it would be considered blasphemous to dance in God!

Not today. It is okay for me to enjoy who I am, and that includes my physicality. I'm not just a brain or floating soul; I'm also a person with a body. How can I appreciate nature or other people if I don't spend time appreciating me?

Today I dance in God with my head held high.

Appeasement

An appeaser is one who feeds a tiger, hoping it will eat him last.
—Winston Churchill

I'm willing to fight for what I believe in. I'm willing to argue for plans that heal abuse and conflict. I will not appease injustice.

Wow. It's hard to believe that I wrote this, and I hope it is true. None of us can really be sure about how we would respond to aggression until our backs are against the wall. However, I'm helped by knowing that aggression feeds on success. If I stand by and let bad things happen to good people, without saying anything, then I could be next. It is in my own interest to fight injustice!

Say Yes to Your Spirit teaches this on a daily basis. I take comfort in the fact that millions believe what I believe.

I will not feed the tiger.

Food

Thou should eat to live, not live to eat.
—Socrates

Say Yes to Your Spirit is about living a positive and creative life. It is realizing that spirituality is more than saying prayers, going to church, and reading the Bible. Spirituality involves being responsible for your body, mind, and feelings.

This must include food: when we eat, what we eat, and how we eat.

I love food. It has always been a source of comfort for me from childhood. I'm fortunate that I like everything, especially cheese!

When I got into recovery from alcoholism I began to look at other compulsive behaviors that I might have, including how I use food. I don't think I'm a food addict, but I need to be responsible in my use of food.

My day goes better if I have breakfast. I feel better. I'm less irritable, more productive. Today my relationship with food is an essential part of my understanding of spirituality.

Today I respect food.

Past

The past is a foreign country; they do things differently there.

—L. P. Hartley

Say Yes to Your Spirit is really about having a positive and creative thought or idea to get us through the day. The above quotation is interesting because it is a different way of talking about the past.

In a sense, the past is over. It has gone. We cannot relive it. I'm not sure that I would describe it as a foreign country, but it's certainly not where we are today. Maybe that is the point. We need to live in the present. Yesterday has gone. We only have today.

So much baggage can be associated with the past, and it is sometimes helpful to let it go and face what is happening now, today. We cannot be present for our dance in God if we are constantly thinking about yesterday.

Today is the beginning of the rest of our lives.

I embrace the moment and
seek to live in the now.

Discovery

To myself I am only a child playing on the beach, while vast oceans of truth lie undiscovered before me.

—Sir Isaac Newton

What a wonderful vision. If we could, on a daily basis, awake with the picture of us playing on a beautiful beach with the vast expanse of the future before us, then I believe fewer people would be depressed, suicidal, and violent.

Say Yes to Your Spirit is the belief that if we really want to, we can change those things that are destructive in our lives. This belief presupposes that we have, within ourselves, the spiritual power to initiate these changes. I believe this. It is called cocreation.

When I place my hand in the hand of God, then I can help heal and remove the pain and suffering that are not only in my life but also in the world.

It is my dance in God.

Are you ready to dance?

On a daily basis, I affirm a positive vision in my life.

Dialogue

In this century, through dialogue, we can live fuller, more compassionate lives.
—Gandhi

I love the vision of me dancing in God. I have steps to make that lead to my joy, happiness, and success. And so do you. Your steps will probably not be the same as mine. However, there is unity in our diversity.

As in dancing, so in speaking; we have a dialogue. My words and your words may not be the same, but if the intention is universal health and wellness, then there will be a unity of spirit.

The tragedy comes when I do not share my dance with you and you also dance alone. When I keep my words for my people and you stay on your side of the street, there is now division . . . and separation.

Say Yes to Your Spirit is celebrating a universal dialogue that celebrates our diversity.

Today I can enjoy the differences that exist in God's creation.

Repercussions

When two elephants fight, it is the grass that gets trampled.

—African Proverb

I've just finished reading a wonderful book called *The Four Agreements* by Don Miguel Ruiz. He has a chapter on the integrity of the word where he explains that what we say or don't say can have repercussions, not only in my life, but also the lives of others. Words can hurt and shame, disempowering people. Words can also charm, enhance, and bring joy to so many people.

This is so true. Only recently have I come to fully understand how I can damage or nurture other people, affecting the energy of the planet.

Say Yes to Your Spirit is the action of living a spiritual life that affords dignity and respect to all people, regardless of class or creed. But more than this, it respects and is mindful of the energy in the universe. My life is important and can be used as a vehicle for God's love. This is my dance in God.

I realize that my words and actions affect the planet.

Fanatics

A fanatic is one who can't change his mind and won't change the subject.
—Winston Churchill

I meet people who say the following:

- Only Christians are going to heaven.
- Gay people are child molesters.
- I know what God wants for God's people. The Bible says it clearly.
- Wives should obey their husbands.
- Jews are Christ killers.

It's hard to discuss anything with a fanatic. I called my book addressing religious addiction and religious abuse *When God Becomes a Drug*. Fanatics seem to be "shooting up" with their words of hate, becoming ever more delusional.

Say Yes to Your Spirit always seeks inclusion and reconciliation.

I accept the differences in this world,
and I celebrate diversity.

Powerlessness

Descartes said, "I think, therefore I am."
He forgot to mention the other part.
"I don't think, therefore I'm not."
—Katagiri Roshi

Alcoholism removed my spiritual power. Alcoholism made my life unmanageable. It is a disease that affects the body, mind, and emotions—the spiritual self. A friend who is in recovery says, "We were walking ghosts. We were there, but not really."

Descartes' famous saying, *Cogito ergo sum* (I think, therefore I am), is so true, but it's hard to think or do anything useful when you are drunk or high.

Since I got sober I've been able to achieve many things because I'm present, not only *in* my life, but *for* life. It is hard to negotiate life when you are not there.

Today I hear birds sing. I see the clouds, and I'm ready to greet the day.

I'm eager for my dance in God.

Holistic

May the outward and inward man be one.

—Socrates

The key to living *Say Yes to Your Spirit* is to have our outsides match our insides. We are connected.

Before I got into recovery I remember trying desperately to "look" okay when I felt terrible. It really is exhausting trying to be something that you do not feel. It is the opposite of being real.

If I feel sad today, I show it or talk to somebody about it. Most days I'm happy in my life, and the smile I reveal to the world is real.

That's why I'm dancing in God.

I am joyous in knowing that
I can reveal my feelings.

Beauty

Beauty is the purgation of superfluities.
—Michelangelo

I remember watching an old man chipping away at a lump of wood, and within minutes it began to take on a shape: the shape of a face. It was not long before the face appeared as a beautiful woman with flowing hair . . . beauty, all in a matter of minutes.

Say Yes to Your Spirit is about creativity. The old man used his skill and imagination to create something from a chunk of wood. In a sense we do that with our lives. We create a life and opportunities to work, meet friends, travel, and possibly help other people.

God has given us a life, and we must decide what we want to do with it. In a sense, God the Creator has created you and me to create. Just like the old man took the wood and made it into something beautiful, so you and I can take our lives and make something beautiful with them and through them.

I am determined to create
a life of beauty.

Simplicity

Simplicity is making the journey of this life with just enough baggage.

—C. D. Warner

We all have baggage in our lives. *Say Yes to Your Spirit* is about keeping the baggage that is necessary and throwing away what we do not need. Easier said than done!

It requires a thorough examination of our past: what happened, what was said, what we did or didn't do. Only when we have exhaustively looked into our lives will we know what we need and what we don't need.

Some years ago I let go of alcohol. I also let go of the church in which I grew up. I moved from England to America. So many other things I determined to let go to live a simpler life: less busy, more focused.

What about you? Are you overwhelmed? Stressed? Working harder rather than smarter? Maybe you need to simplify your life to be more effective.

I seek simplicity in my life.

Patriotism

Patriotism is supporting your country all the time and the government when it deserves it.
—Mark Twain

Say *Yes to Your Spirit* involves the concept of love, including love of country. But as Mark Twain suggests, this does not mean that we agree with everything that is said or done in our country. Healthy patriotism means that sometimes we should be critical of civic or governmental laws. The history of any country is the history of debates, disagreements, and protest, and we in recovery are not unaffected. In my dance in God, I realize that I have a civic responsibility to vote, write to my congressperson, and sometimes march to protest an idea or legislation.

This does not mean that I'm right and other people are wrong. Rather I am celebrating freedom of speech and expressing, in safety, what I think or feel.

I thank God for democracy.

Envy

Envy is the ulcer of the soul.
—Socrates

For years I was envious of other people. I always wanted to be somebody else, to have what they had, to live in the style that they lived. I didn't enjoy living in my own skin. The grass was greener on the other side.

Then I went into therapy and began to examine my life: what I did and believed, and who I was as a person. With family and friends I discussed my ideas and feelings, growing in acceptance of myself. It didn't happen overnight. It took time, but I eventually grew to like Leo. I began to love myself.

I still appreciate the lives of others and occasionally want what they have, but most days I'm comfortable in my skin. My *Say Yes to Your Spirit* involves a love and acceptance of myself.

I love myself the way I am.

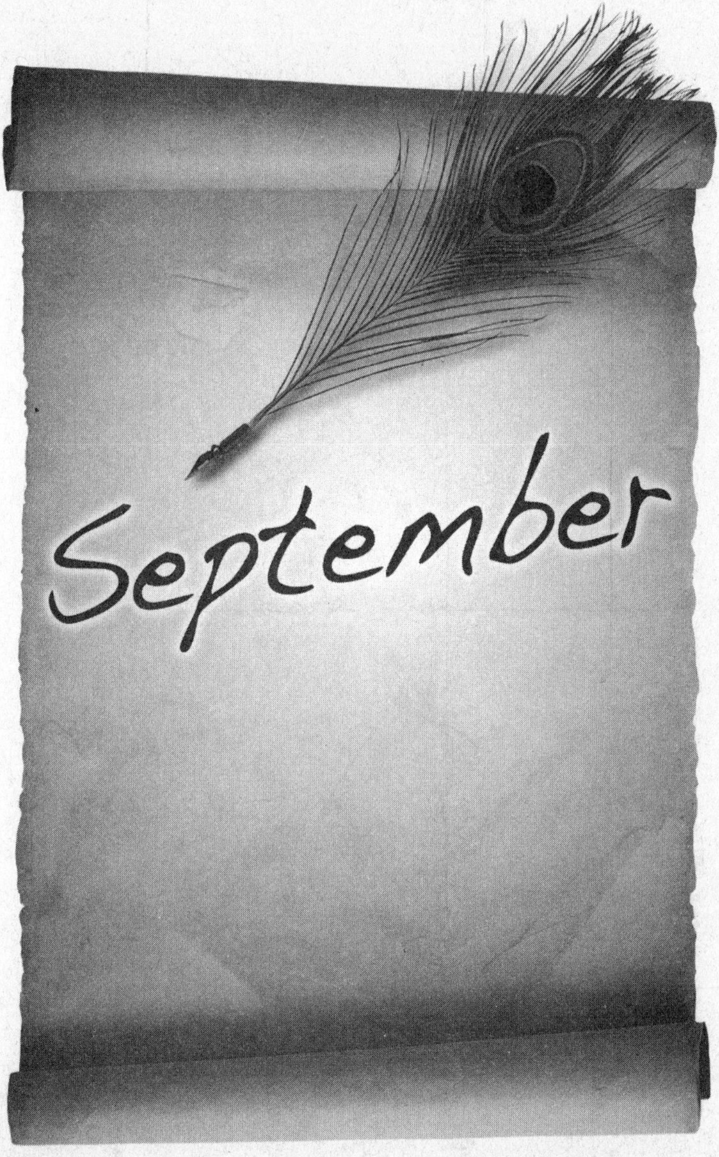
September

Wealth

Being rich is having money; being wealthy is having time.
—Margaret Bonnano

There is an understanding of wealth that is more than having money. It involves peace of mind, friends, love, and having time to simply enjoy life.

W. H. Davies wrote:

What is this life if, full of care,
We have no time to stand and stare?

For too many years I lived to make money, thinking that it would bring happiness. It didn't. Don't get me wrong. Money is important, but so are other things, not least the time to enjoy one's life. I'm discovering that our lives are relatively short and we need to take the time to enjoy . . . enjoy food, friends, nature, and oneself.

Say Yes to Your Spirit brings a wealth that comes with appreciating all that is in this world, enabling our dance in God.

Today I make time
to enjoy my life.

Relationships

I know what I have given you. I do not know what you have received.

—Antonio Porchia

There is always an unknown aspect in any relationship because we know how *we* feel, how *we* think, but can we ever really know what another person is feeling or thinking?

Communication is essential in any relationship; otherwise the unknown can become an aspect of estrangement. Trust enters into the picture here. I can only tell you how I am feeling if I trust you. I can only tell you my innermost thoughts if I trust you.

Therapy is based upon sharing, which in turn is based upon trust.

The best relationships I have known and know are those in which the communication between the people concerned is clear and constant.

I seek to develop relationships that are based upon clear communication.

Humor

Fox hunting is the unspeakable chasing the uneatable.
—Oscar Wilde

Humor is often educational. We can say something that is funny and yet also insightful. Oscar Wilde was famous for his humorous asides:

- "I can resist everything except temptation."
- "What is a cynic? A man who knows the price of everything and the value of nothing."
- "Experience is the name we give to our mistakes."
- "A man cannot be too careful in the choice of his enemies."
- "My wallpaper and I are fighting a duel to the death. One or the other of us has got to go."

Oscar Wilde's writing makes us think . . . and smile.

I realize in my dance in God that
God is often laughing.

War

A great war leaves the country with three armies: an army of cripples, an army of mourners, and an army of thieves.

—German Proverb

Say Yes to Your Spirit dares to envision a world without wars. They are not inevitable. People make war; ideas do not make war!

People who are embracing recovery from drugs or alcohol have made the conscious decision to change a behavior in their lives. I made the decision not to use alcohol, and I surround myself with supportive people. Friends made the decision not to use drugs, and they surround themselves with supportive people. This is a model for stopping war.

Say Yes to Your Spirit envisions world leaders saying publicly that they have made the decision not to use war as a tool for the assertion of ideas, and these leaders surround themselves with supportive diplomats and government officials.

I pray for world peace
on a daily basis.

Society

In a consumer society there are inevitably two kinds of slaves: the prisoners of addiction and the prisoners of envy.
—Ivan Illich

If we talk about dancing in God, then we envision a joyous society, a kingdom of heaven on earth. Why? Because it's really impossible to be festive, to dance, if the atmosphere is polluted with anger, addiction, and envy.

For this reason I bring before you the idea of *Say Yes to Your Spirit*, which is based on respect, tolerance, and the celebration of diversity.

Addiction, which is really another way of talking about a lack of balance, not only destroys a life, but if left untreated it can destroy a society. Envy is a lack of personal self-esteem and the destruction of others. No society can survive such consistent and widespread behaviors.

We need to be respectful and balanced consumers.

I seek to live my life in moderation.

Judgment

I ask you to judge me by the enemies I have made.

—Franklin Delano Roosevelt

When we talk about spirituality we often give the impression that it is wrong to judge another; being judgmental is a negative.

Well, yes, we understand that it is not helpful if you spend all your time knocking other people down and being judgmental toward those who are different. However, truth to tell, we all make judgments. Life without judgments is a life of chaos.

We all have judged Hitler and found him to be a criminal. We judge abusers and suggest treatment and healing. All laws are aspects of judgment.

Say Yes to Your Spirit is about making judgments that reflect how we would want to be judged. When I reflect upon my own life, I discover that my judgments are often tinged with forgiveness.

There but for the grace of God go I.

Today I try to understand the people I am judging.

Truth

During times of universal deceit, telling the truth becomes a revolutionary act.

—George Orwell

Gosh, it's really hard to tell the truth all the time. I know I don't . . . for many reasons.

- I'm afraid what you might think of me.
- I'm trying to protect the people I love.
- I don't trust.
- I want to please other people.

However, I do believe that being honest and truthful is the key to *Say Yes to Your Spirit*. Dancing in God is hard if you are hiding from other people in deceit and manipulation.

It really takes courage to be truthful. As George Orwell says, it's almost a revolutionary act because most people are just like me.

I pray that I can become a revolutionary for truth.

Appearance

A fly that lands on a carabao feels itself to be higher than the carabao.

—Filipino Proverb

I've always believed that appearance is directly connected to self-esteem. Sometimes, when I'm feeling a little low or slightly depressed, I'll go out and buy a shirt or jacket. Wearing good clothes helps me feel better.

Occasionally I'll get a haircut, and I feel younger and fresher.

Even the thought of knowing I'm wearing a good watch helps me give a better talk.

I read in a style magazine that we are what we look. I don't really believe this, but I do think that how we feel about our appearance makes for a certain style.

Say Yes to Your Spirit involves style, and style definitely involves our appearance—how we want to greet the day.

Today I believe that we are as young as we appear.

Hatred

Hatred—the anger of the weak.

—Alphonse Daudet

I've never really been an angry person. I do remember, though, that my father could get very angry, sometimes enraged, and it usually involved my mother. If she ever said anything that made him appear weak, then his defense was anger. It was a sad situation for many years because my mother seemed to take a sick glee in saying things that made my father angry. Thank God, after many years, they seemed to get over this unhealthy cyclic behavior.

Hatred is perhaps the next stage beyond anger and rage. I've always felt that a hateful person was insecure—against homosexuals, minorities, people who are different. Hateful people never seem comfortable in their own skins, so they take their feelings of low self-esteem out on others.

I'm so pleased that I'm in recovery, dealing with my personality defects on a daily basis.

Today I avoid hateful people.

Detachment

Irreverence is the champion of liberty and its only sure defense.
—Mark Twain

Irreverence is an unusual word because so often it can mean disrespect. A person who insults the beliefs or behaviors of another is often referred to as "irreverent."

But as with so much that we have discussed in this book, words can have many meanings and usages. Mark Twain is referring to a type of irreverence that verges on detachment. It is dangerous to be so involved in an idea that you cannot discuss it *objectively*, and sometimes a little irreverence gives an idea a certain perspective, especially when it comes to religious opinions.

Say Yes to Your Spirit is able to consider the funny aspects of being human. When we dance in God, we don't need to take ourselves too seriously; detachment is a necessary spiritual value.

Today I can look at life with a spiritual detachment.

Arrogance

I distrust those people who know so well what God wants them to do, because I notice it always coincides with their own desires.
—Susan B. Anthony

Some years ago, when I was more religious than I am today, I had a certain arrogance that was bolstered by my religious convictions. Usually these convictions were in my own interest; I was definitely the beneficiary.

- Being a Christian, I felt that Christianity was the truest religion.
- Being European, I felt that Europe was more civilized than any other continent.
- I'm white, and so I had an investment in many racist remarks.

Of course, I was insecure. I hadn't traveled much, and I knew little of other cultures.

When I moved out of my religious and cultural box, I was able to appreciate spirituality.

Today I believe there are many paths to God.

Doubt

The problem with the world is that fools and fanatics are always so certain of themselves, and wiser people so full of doubts.

—Bertrand Russell

As I get older I'm discovering that I have more doubts about life, religion, and morality. I used to be so sure about so many things, but now I'm finding that I'm agnostic about so much.

According to Bertrand Russell, doubt makes me a wiser person, but it is also strangely painful.

- I'm not so sure about what happens after death.
- Religion seems to create as many problems as possible answers.
- Moral issues that seemed crystal clear are now foggy at best.

Say Yes to Your Spirit embraces the doubt and the pain. Life brings conflicts, and *wanting* everything to be black and white doesn't make it so.

When I dance in God, I'm not always sure where I'm going.

I'm trying to make my doubts less painful.

Contempt

Wrongs are often forgiven, but contempt never is. Our pride remembers it forever.
—Lord Chesterfield

I was a young boy walking to school with some Jewish friends, and we were attacked by a group of neo-Nazis. They pushed us to the ground and started to hit us, shouting, "dirty Jews." I'm not Jewish, but simply by association I was involved . . . and so very afraid. I'd never seen contempt on a face before, and I will never forget it.

Where does contempt live? It lives in racists, homophobes, religious bigots, sexists, and xenophobes.

Where does it come from? It comes from insecurity and lies, lies told to us when we were young. People are taught to hate.

Say Yes to Your Spirit is about bringing people together, not keeping them apart. It is about respecting difference rather than expecting everyone to be the same.

Spirituality is the antidote to contempt.

I seek to envision a world
that respects difference.

Knowledge

Those who cannot remember the past are condemned to repeat it.
—George Santayana

I belong to a fellowship that asks its members to remember what it was like, what happened, and what it is like now. My past is nothing like the present.

- I was a religious bigot.
- I was a snob.
- I was racist.
- I feared people who were different.
- I drank too much.
- I spent money foolishly.
- I was not dependable.

Today I do not live in the past; why would I want to do such a thing? It was not a happy life, but I need to remember it.

I believe you can only heal and change what you know; ignorance is death.

I can change if I'm prepared to remember.

Life

The best things in life are nearest: breath in your nostrils, light in your eyes, flowers at your feet, duties at your hand, the path of right just before you.

—Robert Louis Stevenson

It is hard to believe that the above quotation came from the mind that wrote *Dr. Jekyll and Mr. Hyde* . . . but maybe not. Life always brings a shadow!

Say Yes to Your Spirit is about seeking the positive things in life and realizing that we can always be creative. It is also about serenity. Another word for "serenity" is "peace," and usually that feeling is accompanied by silence.

A successful life is about appreciating the small things in life—the things that can be easily taken for granted.

- A friend's telephone call
- A bowl of hot soup
- The smell of fresh bread
- A child's smile
- The cool wind on your face

We all know there is a shadow in life, but sometimes we want to spend a moment in the light.

Today I remember the small things that I often take for granted.

Conflict

It is only those who have neither fired a shot nor heard the shrieks and groans of the wounded who cry aloud for blood, more vengeance, more desolation. War is hell.

—General W. T. Sherman

Say Yes to Your Spirit is always about reality. Life is not always what we would want it to be. As I write this book there are conflicts in Afghanistan, Iraq, the Middle East, and Somalia. War is still rearing its ugly head in many parts of the world.

Yet there is also peace in most of the world. Different people with different cultures and religions are living alongside each other in peace. This is how the world is: most people are living in peace, if not prosperity. Some people are at war and poor.

Will it ever change? Yes it will, if *we* change.

War is hell. We need to speak this truth and bring peace to our world.

I am working to heal the conflicts in the world.

Privacy

If privacy is outlawed, only outlaws will have privacy.
—Phil Zimmerman

When we *Say Yes to Your Spirit* we understand that we all need our private place, our private time when we can be alone with ourselves. Stress will always come into our lives if we do not create a quiet place to be still. Remember the psalmist's wise words, "Be still and know that I am God."

This is easier said than done: I'm too busy; I'm fearful that I will not have enough money for my retirement; I rush to please people whom I hardly know or care about. At times it is crazy, stressful.

Then I read about privacy. I know that I need to be a king in my own castle, and maybe that thought will lead to action.

I'm glad I know that sometimes
I need to be alone.

Love

A heart set on love will do no wrong.

—Confucius

I wish this were true. I know that my heart is set on love, but I do things that I do not like; things that are shameful.

Say Yes to Your Spirit understands that I am not perfect. Even though I seek to be positive and creative in my life, I also know that at times I do things that are destructive and negative.

Why? I am human. Also, at times I get with people who lead me astray. I need books like this one, so that each day I can read something that will be helpful in my life.

Thank God I believe in a Higher Power that is accepting, loving, and forgiving.

Because I have this God in my life, I'm able to dance . . . imperfectly.

I have a love that
is not perfect.

Generosity

I am in the habit of looking not so much to the nature of a gift as to the spirit in which it is offered.

—G. K. Chesterton

I try to be generous today because I'm grateful for all the many blessings in my life. I have been given so much that I need to share with others.

I didn't always feel like this. For many years I was selfish, not willing to share money or feelings. It was during those drinking days when I was lost in anger and self-pity. But I've changed. *Say Yes to Your Spirit* is celebrating the fact that millions of people, like me, have changed for the better.

I don't just consider the value of the gift. Today, I'm aware of the intention. A smile and a hug can be the most valuable demonstrations of love that I receive in any given day.

Creative Spirit, I'm so glad that you gave me the power to change.

Dysfunction

Those to whom evil is done do evil in return.
—W. H. Auden

I understand today that if you were the victim of abuse as a child you could easily grow up to be an abuser.

Alcoholics create alcoholics.

Womanizers produce sons who follow in their footsteps.

Racists nurture racists.

This is not always true; indeed, I know people who were so disgusted by the attitudes they experienced in their homes that they marched in the opposite direction. But it certainly seems to be proven in statistic after statistic that we are influenced by our family, especially in childhood.

If *Say Yes to Your Spirit* is about influencing people at an early age to love, forgive, and accept people who are different and rejoice in religious diversity, then we create a better world through influence. What better place to start than when people are young?

I treat the mind of a young person with great respect.

Family

The most important thing a father can do for his children is to love their mother.
—Theodore Hesburgh

My parents died at ninety-one, six months apart. They were married for sixty-six years. My father always loved and showed his affection toward my mother.

- He would buy her flowers every month, even when they had little money.
- They held hands, and he always made sure she was on the inside when they walked down the street.
- He always asked her opinion.
- Every night they prayed each prayer together, followed by a kiss.

Respect! My father respected my mother. He respected and showed his respect for women. He believed in equality even when it was not popular in England.

And this has influenced me.

I have great respect for women, especially ministers in religious denominations.

Family and relationships require respect.

Art

There is one art, no more, no less; to do all things with artlessness.
—Piet Hein

Art is the opposite of pretension; it is always *real.* I suppose for this reason it is often seen as a gift.

- The young boy who plays the piano so naturally.
- The graceful movements of dancers when they are not dancing.
- An uneducated person who has an incredible way with words.
- The singer who has never had a singing lesson.

I suppose you could call it "being natural." I believe this is the way to live *Say Yes to Your Spirit*: do what comes naturally. I believe that goodness, forgiveness, love, and laughter are the way God intended us to live. If we could only let go of the pretension that is making us appear and sound false, then everything would be bliss, the way life was intended to be.

I appreciate and cultivate art in my life.

Maturity

Born to be wild—live to outgrow it.

—Lao-tzu

A friend of mine who is in his late fifties told me recently that he can't wait to grow up! I know what he means. In so many ways I still seem to be irresponsible and immature.

However, I do understand that spirituality involves being mature, taking responsibility for our lives and always showing respect to other people. In the movie *Arthur*, the butler says, "Arthur, it's time to grow up. You can't always be a drunk. You need to become responsible."

This is good advice. I need to hear it. What about you?

- What do you need to change in your life to be more responsible?
- What habit or behaviors do you need to let go of?
- How are you with money . . . and shopping?
- Do you connect maturity with responsibility?

Today I do not connect maturity with being old.

Health

Your body is precious. It is our vehicle for awakening. Treat it with care.
—Gautama Buddha

Say Yes to Your Spirit has an emphasis upon taking care of the whole person, which includes our bodies. Religious people have historically paid attention to saying prayers and reading their Bibles, but they often forget the "temple of the spirit."

Today my dance in God includes:

- A walk on the beach
- Vegetables
- Rest
- Three pints of water a day
- And cheese!

When I am healthy, I feel so energized. This affects everything that I do. For too many years I did not treat my body with respect. Today I love my body, and it shows.

My Say Yes to Your Spirit
includes broccoli.

Children

If you want your children to turn out well, spend twice as much time with them, and half as much money.

—Abigail van Buren

Codependency was a hot topic some years ago, and I believe it is still a serious problem in our society. Nearly every dysfunctional family has a dose of codependency.

Parents who are in recovery often tell me that they felt so guilty about how they behaved as alcoholics and drug addicts, especially regarding the treatment of their children, that they tried to buy love. Guilt produced a lavish overindulgence toward their children, who became spoiled brats!

We all need love and affection. Money is no substitute for a gentle hug, a smile, and occasionally a severe reprimand.

Today I'm able to love without seeking to purchase it.

Justice

Everything secret degenerates, even the administration of justice; nothing is safe that does not show how it can bear discussion and publicity.

—Lord Acton

Jesus talked about bringing our problems to "the light." Today we are asked to consider the thought that justice cannot be served if it is secret.

The history of any government usually reveals that when laws are administered by a few, without debate or discussion, crimes are committed—in the name of the law.

This is also true for individuals. If we believe that an injustice has been served upon us, then we need to be able to take our case before an open court of opinion. Secrecy only serves to make bad laws even more abusive.

Say Yes to Your Spirit proposes that life in any part of society needs to exist in the light.

Today I will not hide my issues from public scrutiny.

Morality

Whenever A attempts by law to impose his moral standards upon B, A is most likely the scoundrel.
—H. L. Mencken

I do not wish to impose my views about spirituality or morality upon other people. Why? Because over the years I have changed my mind about so many things!

Also, personally, I do not like it when anybody tries to force me to accept what he or she believes is the right way to live. I love freedom. I love my freedom.

Of course I accept that we need to abide by certain accepted laws in our society, but I still have a large area of my life that is free; this is my understanding of *Say Yes to Your Spirit.*

I want to dance in God, but I do not want to force *you* to dance in my steps. You must be allowed to create your own dance.

I cherish the word "freedom."

Government

Governing a great nation is like cooking a small fish. Do not overdo it.

—Lao-tzu

I love the 12-step program because it does not force opinions on religion, government, or morality down my throat. It celebrates the concept that we must all live and let live. It clearly affirms that suggestions are not laws, and leaders are only trusted servants.

And it works for many different people with different backgrounds and religions. If more governments and countries lived with the philosophy of the 12-step program, I believe there would be less war and fewer conflicts and acts of aggression.

Say Yes to Your Spirit seeks to incorporate the 12 steps into its philosophy, and then we can all really dance!

I need to have freedom of expression
if I am to dance in God.

Recovery

No matter how far you have gone on the wrong road, turn back.

—Turkish Proverb

I used to be a drunk . . . and then I stopped drinking.

Other people used to take drugs . . . and they stopped.

Still others were sex addicts . . . and they changed.

The list is endless. But undeniably people can change, at *any* age.

Recently I met a lady in her eighties who had been an alcoholic for most of her life. She had lost everything and everyone whom she had loved. Two years ago, she stopped drinking. Her life changed. Today she is happy and has regained the respect of the people she loved.

What about you? Are you ready to change, or do you want to wait until you are eighty?

I don't intend to waste my life.

Certainty

If a man will begin with certainties, he shall end in doubts; but if he will be content to begin with doubts, he shall end in certainties.

—Francis Bacon

Only when I was willing to express my doubts about life, religion, and God did I develop a spirituality that is firm and secure.

Years ago I gave the impression that I was certain about so many things, but it was a pretense. I felt I was a stronger person if I always knew things . . . and so I raised my voice!

Today I know that I do not know many things, and this expression of my doubts has made me a stronger person.

Today I'm able to live with a *Say Yes to Your Spirit* that permits doubts.

I'm happy in my dance in God,
even though my steps
are uncertain.

October

Education

A man who has never gone to school may steal from a freight car; but if he has a university education, he may steal the whole railroad.
—Theodore Roosevelt

A friend of mine who is a policeman told me that to be a really good detective you need to think like a criminal. The more that you know about something, the more you can understand it.

I understand alcoholism. Indeed, it is the awareness of my disease that helped me move into recovery. In a strange way the disease is the doorway to health!

Recently, I was giving a lecture, and we had written up on the board six symptoms of alcoholism. I told the group that the opposite feelings or actions are the symptoms of recovery. For example:

Denial	Acceptance
Anger/Rage	Peace
Dishonesty	Honesty
Violence	Gentleness
Shame	Freedom
Isolation	Involvement

What I experience is not a waste of time.

Inspiration

My aim is to agitate and disturb people.
I'm not selling bread, I'm selling yeast.
—Miguel de Unamuno y Jugo

Spiritual people sometimes say things that upset people.

Jesus said, "Leave the dead to bury the dead."

Gautama Buddha remarked, "Money can be the door to grief."

Gandhi declared, "An eye for an eye makes the whole world blind."

The above statements make us think. We are inspired when we think, when we understand what needs to be done: when we have awareness.

The purpose of this book is to start the day with a thought, sentence, or word that will help each of us to be a better person. Not that we are ever really bad—however, we are creating something that otherwise might not happen. We are dancing in God because there is a sense in which we are "godlings" on earth, initiators of love. We who are inspired also inspire.

I seek inspiration every day.

Facts

Facts do not cease to exist because they are ignored.
—Aldous Huxley

For many years I lived in denial. I did not want to face what was happening in my life: alcoholism. Only when I faced the music and understood the facts could I change.

Say Yes to Your Spirit is about knowing the spiritual facts: we can change our lives. Emphasis is on the "we."

I do not believe that God gets people sober. God *wants* alcoholics to be sober, but we must want it too. Waiting for God's grace is a waste of time.

The fact is that God has given us the power to change our lives. Do we want to change? Do we want to use the power that we have?

When we look into history and study the lives of men and women who have changed the world for the better, they all *did* something. This is a spiritual fact.

The facts of life are spiritual.

Thinking

People rarely win wars, governments rarely lose them.
—Arundhati Roy

Say Yes to Your Spirit is a willingness to think differently, making an effort to improve the world and our lives.

Wars still exist, and they cause havoc to the people involved.

- Thousands die.
- Houses are destroyed.
- Children live in fear.
- Business opportunities are decimated.

Why? The havoc is because of greed, disagreements, and fear. So many reasons are given, but few of them really make sense.

Is there any other way? Yes. If we are prepared to dance in God, then we appreciate the natural joy that comes with life; then we appreciate the beauty of this world and the people who are in it. War would only be the very last resort.

When I prepare myself to think,
then I become responsible.

Strategy

Knowing ignorance is strength; ignoring knowledge is sickness.
—Lao-tzu

When I know that I do not know, then I am smarter. When I pretend to know something that I don't, I lose.

For too many years I pretended to be what I was not, and it was a painful period in my life. Denial is a relatively short word with long consequences.

Say Yes to Your Spirit is being honest. What I do not know will rarely hurt me. What I do know can bring me success. I know that I am an alcoholic, and I do not drink. I know that God's power is within me, and I create a wonderful life. I value the differences that are in this world, and I am richer for it. I know that friendship is an aspect of love, and I have many friends.

Now you know why I'm dancing.

Ignorance is rarely bliss.

Freedom

I love my country too much to be a nationalist.

—Albert Camus

Say Yes to Your Spirit is always about balance. Throughout this book we have talked about the danger of addiction to alcoholism, drugs, sex, and food. But there is also the addiction to being right or being better than other people. Nationalism, if not balanced by a respect for other cultures, can be dangerous.

When we dance in God, we are really dancing with the universe, enjoying everything that makes for a happy life. This is the key to spiritual living, and it is based on the Golden Rule: treat other people the way you would want to be treated.

I love my country. I love my culture. I also, however, have a deep and growing respect for other countries and their cultures.

This all makes for a deeper and richer life.

Freedom is the basis of
Say Yes to Your Spirit.

Wonderment

Trees are the earth's endless effort to speak to the listening heaven.
—Rabindranath Tagore

I met a lady the other day who told me that she was a pantheist. I had to look it up in the dictionary. I discovered that "pantheism" is a belief that Nature is divine. Some pantheists suggest that Nature is God.

I know I am not a pantheist, but I do have a deep and abiding respect, even wonderment, with regard to nature. I love the forest and trees.

Say Yes to Your Spirit reminds us that God is to be discovered in nature. We've already suggested in this book that spirituality and religion are not the same, and many people are fed spiritually by nature. They have never been able to truly find God in a church, but when they stand on a mountain or walk beside the ocean they feel the presence of God.

Nature is their temple. Nature is their sacred space.

I know that nature reflects
the glory of God.

Egotism

Egotism is the anesthetic that dulls the pain of stupidity.

—Frank William Leahy

I know that it is important to have a healthy ego, and I must confess that it is easier said than done! Why? Well, I often think that people should think or believe what I think and believe. I know what I want in my life, and I tend to expect other people to want the same things. This can make me not a little arrogant!

But I know this today: an unhealthy ego is a character defect that I need to battle on a daily basis. Each day I attempt to tell myself that other people have different ideas and beliefs—and this makes for a richer world. Variety really is the spice of life.

Keeping this balance in my life is part of my *Say Yes to Your Spirit*, and it is one of the spiritual steps I need to remember in my dance in God.

I respect my ego. I also respect the ego of other people.

Intuition

Every man is a volume if you know how to read him.
—William Ellery

I believe that when we take care of our bodies, inform our minds, and express our emotions, we become healthy people. We develop a healthy energy that is spiritual.

If we continue to live a healthy life, we will also develop the power of intuition or insight. I see this in the life of Jesus, and I am sure it existed in Gautama Buddha and other spiritual men and women. But it can also be developed in us.

When we dance in God, we also see with the eyes of God. We see beyond the surface into the minds and hearts of other people. Naturally this will make our decisions better and healthier. We become our own prophets. We become our own seers.

Jesus said it so beautifully, "Having eyes, do you not see?"

Today, I see with the eyes of God.

Achievement

Great acts are made up of small deeds.

—Lao-tzu

A friend asked me recently, "How do you get sober? And how do you stay sober?"

- Go to AA meetings.
- Get a sponsor.
- Read books on recovery.
- Sit at the front of the meeting.
- Don't have alcohol in your house.
- Eat three meals a day.
- Avoid gossip.
- Go to bed early.
- Say your prayers, *but* remember to move your feet.
- Work the 12 steps.

None of this is difficult. It is harder to stay drunk than it is to get sober!

Being a drunk is a very hard life.

It's easier to stay healthy than it is to get sick.

Education

Everything is for the eyes these days—TV, "Life," "Look," the movies. Nothing is just for the mind. The next generation will have eyeballs as big as cantaloupes and no brain at all.

—Fred Allen

When I was talking to a friend I caught myself saying, "in the good old days." Suddenly I sounded like my mother, just before she died at age ninety-one!

I truly believe that things are getting better in life, including education. However, knowledge is different. Pictures have replaced print. Young people know more and have access to information through the Internet, and it is good.

Say Yes to Your Spirit affirms the future, which includes education. Truly I believe that the past is the seedbed for the future and that the future will be a spiritual adventure.

We are dancing in God; this statement would not have made sense fifty years ago.

I am an optimist when it comes to the future.

Insight

A person usually has two reasons for doing something: a good reason and the real reason.
—Thomas Carlyle

When I was drinking alcohol I told many lies to cover what was happening in my life. Then I decided to embark on a spiritual journey and get real.

When I *Say Yes to Your Spirit* I seek to be honest, giving the real reason that I say and do things. This is not always easy, because not everything I say or do is spiritual. However, honesty keeps me on the spiritual path.

I can only dance in God when I am honest; dishonesty separates me from God. No matter how good the reason for dishonesty sounds, it is still a lie.

What about you? Are you able to connect honesty with living the spiritual life?

I do not feel comfortable when
I am being dishonest.

Influence

Don't ask me who's influenced me. A lion is made up of the lambs he's digested, and I've been reading all my life.

—Giorgos Seferis

I have been influenced by many people. Most of them I never met. I read about them, what they have said or done. Like Giorgos, I am a voracious reader.

When I *Say Yes to Your Spirit* I acknowledge the power of influence in my life, and I intend it to be positive. Why? Because for too many years I was influenced by negative people, my so-called drinking buddies!

My mother used to say, "Leo, you are easily led." She meant that I could be influenced by destructive people. She was right.

Today I avoid negative people and begin my day with a positive reading or thought. It works.

I am not going to allow negative thoughts or people in my life.

Spirituality

If you don't find God in the next person you meet, it is a waste of time looking for him further.
—Gandhi

I believe that all people carry something of God within them. However, sometimes you must look very hard to see God!

A man who comes to the support meetings I attend always seems angry. Quite frankly, I avoid him. One day he was getting coffee, and I stood silently to the side.

"Can I get you a coffee, Leo?" he asked.

"Thank you. I didn't know you knew my name."

"Yes, I know you. I've heard you speak, but I'm normally very shy," he replied. "My therapist is helping me reach out."

What I thought was anger was really fear.

Today I believe that if I *really know you*, really know you, I would love you. I would discover that part of you that is God.

The reign of God is within us.

Wisdom

He who knows does not speak. He who speaks does not know.

—Lao-tzu

We are not expected to take this saying literally; rather we are to seek the wisdom in the paradox.

Say Yes to Your Spirit is about having many balls in the air at the same time. It always embraces the wisdom of diversity. Why? There are many paths to God, just as there are many ways of dancing in God; some are religious and others are not. There are different ways of speaking about God or praying to God. Spirituality includes the light and the darkness.

If we take a moment to look around at our world we still see that it has been created in variety, difference. This is the clue to speaking about the Creator.

More is always being revealed.

Today my spiritual journey is important, not the destination.

Conversation

What is reading but silent conversation?

—Walter Savage Landor

Say Yes to Your Spirit involves appreciation, and I sometimes take conversation for granted. Like the air we breathe or the water we drink, conversation has always been in my life. Occasionally, when I go for a day or more without seeing anyone, which is extremely rare, then I miss conversation.

Conversation is really connection—people sharing ideas or giving information that allows those people to be known. When I share my story at a recovery meeting, I am really having a one-way conversation with the crowd. I allow them to know me.

Reading a book takes me into the mind of the author; also I can get to know more about myself. I hope this book is helping you, not only to get to know me, but also to know more about yourself.

Good conversation always leads to awareness.

When I dance in God, I am having a silent conversation.

Connection

Your children need your presence more than your presents.
—Jesse Jackson

A friend said to me recently, "A spoiled child is an abused child." He continued, "When you give them too much, you actually hurt them. They come to expect things in life, rather than earning them."

I think this is what Jesse Jackson meant. The greatest gifts you can give a child are your love and your presence.

I was a spoiled child. I was the younger, and my parents gave me everything: money, education, trips abroad; they also gave me love. However, for many years I expected people to do things for me or appreciate me in a special way. But I was not everybody's younger son!

Today I know that it was my parents' love that I needed. All children require love.

Love is the greatest gift.

I am loved, and I give love.

Security

It is always the secure who are humble.

—G. K. Chesterton

Father Kevin Taylor, a friend of mine, often says that insecure people are dangerous. He is right.

When I was drinking I was very insecure. This insecurity hurt me and other people I loved.

Why was I insecure? Because alcoholism makes you feel powerless in your life and everything seem unmanageable:

- You become unreliable.
- You are angry at yourself, and you transfer this anger to other people.
- You act as if everything is okay, but inside you are hurting.
- Your energy is dissipated.

All the above make you feel insecure. Oh yes, and you feel separated from God's love.

In recovery I have found security, and my gratitude for sobriety has helped me become humble.

My humility is based upon gratitude.

Conscience

When will our consciences grow so tender that we will act to prevent human misery rather than avenge it?

—Eleanor Roosevelt

I read a book about the life of Adolf Eichmann. Even when he was on trial he seemed to have no conscience or awareness of the death, pain, and suffering he had caused. Hitler was said to have acted with the same indifference.

Say Yes to Your Spirit is about nurturing our conscience. We all need to be aware of what we are doing and saying in life because our lives affect other people. Only when we understand that we can love or damage other people will we live noble lives. Our conscience tells us when we are wrong or that we are responsible. Because I have been hurt in my life, I do not want to knowingly hurt anyone.

In recovery I know that this ideal is attainable.

Today I thank God that
I have a conscience.

Sufficiency

He who knows that enough is enough will always have enough.

—Lao-tzu

I am content in my life, because I have enough to make me happy.

This has not been always true. Some years ago I chased happiness. I thought that if I had more money, more houses, more . . . then I would be happy. It nearly killed me.

Then a friend said, "You have all you need."

"What?"

"You have all that you need, inside yourself, to make you happy."

"But if I . . ."

"Shh! Listen. All that you will ever need has been given to you. Seek within."

And he was right. Once I became comfortable with me, then I could feel comfortable with the world.

Today I am happy.

Spring

Autumn is a second spring when every leaf is a flower.
—Albert Camus

I love spring. Everything seems fresh, growing, renewing, resurrecting.

Albert Camus is suggesting that we can find aspects of spring in autumn.

I say throughout this book that metaphor and poetry are essential to understanding *Say Yes to Your Spirit.* With this in mind, I believe that wherever we discover new life, a change for the better, we are experiencing spring.

Recovery from alcoholism, especially if it is connected with a spiritual support program, gives a person permanent spring. The concept of resurrection becomes a living reality, miracle a daily experience.

What about winter and summer? Well, they bring different stories . . . all good.

With spiritual eyes,
everything is wonderful.

Feelings

Other men are lenses through which we read our own minds.

—Ralph Waldo Emerson

Whenever I listen to a person share real feelings I connect to them. Even if they are sharing experiences that I have never had, the feelings are the same. I believe that all human beings are connected through our feelings.

Say Yes to Your Spirit is really very emotional, more than intellectual. A friend of mine recently said that our feelings are the demonstrations of the soul. Thoughts can bring people together, but feelings really connect people.

I once went to a recovery support group in Vietnam. I was the only English-speaking person. I did not understand a word that was spoken, yet the tears and laughter made the connection that I was looking for that night.

When a person honestly shares feelings with another, then the oneness of this world is again revealed.

My shared humanity
is revealed in my feelings.

Company

The first method for estimating the intelligence of a ruler is to look at the men he has around him.

—Niccolo Machiavelli

What company do you keep? What are your friends like?

These are interesting questions. Most of my friends are in recovery. We call each other every week and share feelings: love, joy, fear, even anger.

Also I try to work with people who in their own special way are saying yes to Spirit. I don't want to be around negative or destructive people because they create a dangerous energy that affects me. In my life I surround myself with people who are positive about life and creative in what they do with each day . . . and I am the beneficiary.

What about you? If you really want to be happy and successful, I believe that the company you keep is important.

Today I search out spiritual people to be in my life.

OCTOBER 24

Work

Life without industry is guilt; industry without art is brutality.
—John Ruskin

I love my work. I am not a workaholic because I incorporate enjoyment and relaxation into each day. Indeed often my work is my joy.

I feel sorry for people who hate their jobs because one-third of their week is miserable. *Say Yes to Your Spirit* is about finding happiness in life, which must include the work that we do. What can you do if you hate your job? Find a new one. Don't work just for the money, although money is important. Work at something that brings you satisfaction. Easier said than done! So, work at doing the work you enjoy. It may take time to find the right thing for you, but try to make the search enjoyable.

I am convinced that having a positive attitude can really make a difference in finding and keeping the right job for your life.

I have made my work an art form called education.

Change

If you do not change direction, you may end up where you are heading.
—Lao-tzu

I needed to change. If I continued to be in active addiction to alcohol, then I would die.

I changed. I am alive and happy.

I think we all need to let go of something . . . and then change.

Things to let go:

- A judgmental God
- An unhealthy relationship
- A compulsive relationship with food
- A pessimistic attitude
- A sex addiction
- Racist behavior
- Homophobia

The list could go on and on. What do you need to let go of in your life? Make a list. Decide on an action plan. Begin today.

It is in your own interest.

I am ready for change.
I will take responsibility for the action.

Education

Books are like imprisoned souls till someone takes them down from a shelf and frees them.
—Samuel Butler

Reading brings the world into my life. Education is something that I enjoy and appreciate.

Have I always enjoyed educating myself? Yes. I had teachers at school and university who made study fun, with the exception of the foreign languages. Both teachers that I had for German and French were boring, and today I cannot speak French or German!

I am convinced that education should be fun, and a good teacher will know how to make the subject come alive. This is also true for other things, especially therapy. Always I try to make the topic of spirituality enjoyable.

I hope you are enjoying this book!

Thank you, God, for the adventure that is called education.

Animals

Half the dogs in America will receive Christmas presents this year, yet few of us pause to consider the miserable life of a pig . . . that becomes a Christmas ham.

—Michael Pollan

When I dance in God I am really discovering that the Divine is all around me. This includes animals.

Actually my favorite animal is the pig. When I visit farms I always look to see if they have a pigsty. I even enjoy the smell! I have said that when I retire I will get a pig farm in England or keep a few around to amuse me.

Animals reflect God's unconditional love. Indeed, when a person says that "such and such acted like an animal," I really think that is an insult to animals. In most cases animals behave with greater respect toward life and nature than many people.

If God asked me to return as an animal
I think I would choose to be a pig . . .
the pig that is the farmer's pet!

Old Age

A man is not old until his regrets take the place of dreams.
—Yiddish Proverb

I still have dreams. I usually enjoy each day. I am always thinking of ways to improve my life and make it more enjoyable. I love people. I am fascinated by different cultures and other religions. There is no food that I don't enjoy. All this keeps me young.

Say Yes to Your Spirit is about living every moment, seeking ways to enjoy each day.

When I was drinking alcohol some years ago, I was old before my time. I didn't enjoy people. I judged other cultures mercilessly. I rarely enjoyed my food. I lived in negativity. I was dying in life!

That was then, and this is now. I am getting younger with each year.

What about you?

I am as young as I feel,
and I feel great.

Responsibility

The buck stops here.

—Harry Truman

When we *Say Yes to Your Spirit* the spiritual word "responsibility" becomes very important. Today I take responsibility for my life.

I am not asking God to do things that I need to do for myself.

My health is really my responsibility. If I want to bring change into my life, I need to pray and also move my feet.

Only in recent years have I discovered the spiritual power of being human. With my new understanding of cocreation, I am able to develop a divine plan for my life that includes success and prosperity.

What do I need to do? Show up in my life. If I do the right things for others, then the right things will show up in my life.

I will not blame other people for what is happening in my life.

Life

What you do is of little significance, but it is very important that you do it.
—Gandhi

I am often satisfied by the relatively insignificant things that occur in my life:

- The smell of fresh coffee.
- A good night's sleep.
- The feel of a clean shirt.
- A cool breeze on my face.
- Dental floss.
- A friend's telephone call.
- Cool water.
- A strong shower.
- A toilet that flushes.

All the above improve the quality of my life. They are small in themselves, but important.

If I take care of the small things in my life, then the big things will take care of themselves.

Today I know that life is really about the small things.

Enlightenment

Knowing others is wisdom; knowing yourself is enlightenment.
—Lao-tzu

Remember what the psalmist said, "Be still and know that I am God."

When we begin to journey into knowing God or a Higher Power, we also begin the journey into ourselves. I am beginning to know who Leo is, and I love him. This is the dance.

Years ago I received the religious message that I needed to love other people and focus on others; to love myself or focus on me was selfish. Also I was not to speak about what I could do or my achievements; that was vanity. A priest told me, "If God wants people to know, he will tell them!"

For years I missed me. Then I began to hear a spiritual message: Know thyself. Love thyself. Be thyself.

Only when I began to find Leo did I really find and understand other people and God.

Be still . . .
and know yourself.

November

Power

Mastering others is strength. Mastering yourself is true power.
—Lao-tzu

When I was thinking about writing *Say Yes to Your Spirit* I wanted to explore the idea of God's power living and emanating in our lives. For too many years I seemed to be "begging" and "asking" God to do things for me, but what about the dynamic concept of the reign of God living in me?

This required a change in my thinking. I am not suggesting that we shouldn't pray or occasionally seek a message or revelation in the Scriptures, but I do believe that God has given us all that we need to face any challenges.

I thought for years that to be a good Christian meant that I affirmed God's power, and my role was to grovel in the dust. Today I choose to dance in God, to claim the divine power that has been given to me.

My success has been determined by this change in thinking.

I affirm my God-given power.

Persistence

It does not matter how slowly you move so long as you do not stop.

—Confucius

I'm proud of my spiritual journey over the years:

- I gave up alcohol.
- I made the decision to live in America.
- I developed a healthy relationship with my parents when they were living.
- I had the opportunity to employ people at Spiritual Concepts.
- I developed a deeper understanding of the difference between spirituality and religion.
- I created new friends in different cultures.

The spiritual journey never ends.

What about you? What are you developing in your life to further your understanding of God? How do you seek, on a daily basis, to live the spiritual life?

Together we move forward.

Spirituality is a process, not an event.

Intention

The journey of a thousand miles begins with one step.
—Lao-tzu

Years ago a Jesuit priest told me about the power of intention; you affirm in your mind what you want to create in your life.

"Leo, think about what you want in your life. Vision it. Then plan the steps that will bring that vision into actuality: intention."

I have never forgotten this advice. Small steps lead to great accomplishments. All I need to do is affirm the intention. For example:

- I am writing this book.
- Each day I write a few pages.
- I envision how the book will be read.
- I read it aloud and listen.
- My intention is for clarity in my writing.

I live one day at a time.

Individuality

Work out your own salvation. Do not depend on others.

—Gautama Buddha

There is a phrase in the 12-step program that says, "principles before personalities." For many years I thought that this meant we should not have a personality or be a character, rather a blended mixture of mediocrity.

Then a friend said, "Leo, it says 'principles before personalities,' but it does not say 'principles *instead of* personalities.' You are still a personality. It's okay. Just look at the people in the 12-step program. Believe me, many of them are *real* personalities."

This advice has proven to be invaluable. I need to be my own person, to say what I believe, to express what I feel. My life and opinions are important.

Yes, I need to consider you. But how can I consider your needs if I have not addressed my own?

Jesus said, "Physician, heal thyself."

I celebrate that I am an individual in the company of others.

Respect

Respect yourself and others will respect you.
—Confucius

It seems strange that this needs to be said, but I have discovered that many people do not respect themselves. But can you really *Say Yes to Your Spirit* if you don't respect yourself? Can you really dance in God if you don't respect yourself? I don't think so.

I have just finished writing an article where I talk about the baggage that we all have in our lives, and I have suggested that we need to develop the courage to confront the baggage to heal. Respect and healing are connected. When we begin to heal the aspects of our life that we don't like, then we develop confidence. With confidence comes the respect.

When we begin to feel good about ourselves, then we create a positive energy toward others, which breeds respect. People respect those who are saying *Say Yes to Your Spirit!*

Today I understand that respect
of self is essential.

Patience

Nature does not hurry, yet everything is accomplished.
—Lao-tzu

Have you ever spent time watching a cat? They never seem to be in a hurry, except when chasing a mouse. Then they really move!

Cats have a great message for human beings: don't be in such a hurry. Take your time. Eat slowly. Move softly and nap often.

Say Yes to Your Spirit is about living a life with a spiritual foundation, and having patience is important. Most times, if I can only calm my spirit, I achieve far more than rushing blindly through my life.

The psalmist said, "Be still and know that I am God." Be still.

My dance in God is not a jitterbug; rather it is a calm and graceful waltz.

I embrace the refreshing gift of patience in my life.

Wisdom

Health is the greatest gift, contentment the greatest wealth, faithfulness the best relationship.
—Gautama Buddha

This saying is at the heart of *Say Yes to Your Spirit*, and it needs to be considered in greater detail.

My health is important. How can I do anything if I am sick? There is no real life if I am unhealthy. That is why I take care of my body. I eat healthily and get my rest.

I am content in my life. I enjoy where I live, what I do, and the friends I have. I do not need anything more in my life to make me happy.

Also I am faithful to my understanding of spirituality. It is based upon the Golden Rule: treat people the way that I would want to be treated.

I understand that when I dance in God, I am also dancing in Buddha.

Today I celebrate the wisdom
that is in my life.

The Past

Study the past if you would define the future.
—Confucius

In 12-step programs they often say, "What was it like? What happened? What is it like now?"

How can you know where you are going if you don't know where you have been? This is particularly true if you are an alcoholic and you want to change your behavior.

Say Yes to Your Spirit is about knowing that we are co-creators with God and that with this knowledge we can determine the future. Can we predict *exactly* what will happen? Not really, but by a study of what has been happening in our lives, we are better able to define the future.

I love the vision of dancing in God. I am mindful that to dance freely we need to have some sense of where we are going.

Do you have a sense of where you are going?

I look to the future because
I've studied the past.

Silence

Silence is the source of great strength.

—Lao-tzu

I don't like too much noise. I need silence. Then I can hear myself think.

A friend of mine has a life that is chaotic: money problems, broken relationships, unemployment, and mental stress. He asked for my advice, and I visited him for a few days. I nearly went insane!

The mobile phone was going every few minutes. His television was left on with the volume turned up. He also had a CD playing while he was trying to talk to me.

I told him, "Stop. Switch everything off. Now."

"Everything?"

"Everything. Now."

Silence . . . no noise. . . . We said a short prayer and remained silent for several minutes. Then we talked.

God created the world in silence. If we want to be successful, then we all need times of silence. Be quiet. Think about your life.

My Say Yes to Your Spirit
involves silence.

The Body

To keep the body in good health is a duty. . . . Otherwise we shall not be able to keep our mind strong and clear.

—Gautama Buddha

For too many years the body had been ignored in religious discussions concerning spirituality. In some cases it was considered okay to ignore the body, escape the body, even abuse the body (self-flagellation).

Thank God those days are over. It is difficult to affirm that the body is the temple of the spirit if at the same time we are denying its value.

The Buddha also makes another valuable point: the body has a direct connection with our minds. When we take care of our bodies we are also affirming health toward our minds and emotions. This concept is part of the movement toward holistic medicine.

Today I respect my body.
This allows me to Say Yes to Your Spirit.

Consequences

When anger rises, think of the consequences.
—Confucius

When I was drinking I was an angry man. Some years ago, even when I wasn't drinking, I was an angry man. Why?

There are many reasons. I thought I should be living a more prosperous life. I thought I should be happier. I thought I was working too hard. Always I blamed other people and God.

Only recently have I begun to *Say Yes to Your Spirit.* Today, I understand that I create my life. My partnership with God, which I visualize as dancing in God, implies that I am responsible for my prosperity, my happiness, and my workload. I cannot blame other people for the life that I am living.

With this awareness has come a quiet satisfaction and a growing awareness of what "spirituality" actually means. I am the creator of my life. If I define "spirituality" as being positive and living creatively, then these are the goals I pursue in my life.

I choose not to nurture
anger in my life.

Paradox

The words of truth are always paradoxical.

—Lao-tzu

From the beginning of my theological studies I have been familiar with the concept of paradox: how we hold together two or more seemingly opposite points of view.

- Jesus was fully human and yet divine.
- God is involved in this world and yet detached.
- Christianity respects other world religions and yet it is the "true faith."

We also have the concept of paradox in recovery.

- We need to let go and yet take responsibility.
- We live in the moment and yet plan for the future.
- Are alcoholics recovered or recovering on a daily basis?

Say Yes to Your Spirit understands that when we are dealing with mystery, paradox is essential.

Today I am able to hold different concepts in my mind.

Thinking

We are shaped by our thoughts. We become what we think.
—Gautama Buddha

There is a teaching in popular psychology that suggests that what we affirm we are able to become. What we can visualize we are able to materialize. Thoughts create miracles.

This philosophy is connected to the theory of intention. We need to affirm something for our lives if we are able to make it happen. We are responsible for what happens in our lives. We create the miracle.

I visualized the publication of this book before I started writing it. I had an intention concerning its diversity and inclusiveness. I could see me dancing in the spirit of God.

If you are reading this book, then it all happened!

Today I believe that what I think,
I am able to become.

Confidence

Wheresoever you go, go with all your heart.
—Confucius

Only recently did I understand that the word "enthusiasm" means having God's energy in my life—not only having it, but also *knowing* I had it in my life. This is the key to those who have discovered *Say Yes to Your Spirit*. It is the awareness that God is within each and every one of us, and with this knowledge comes divine power.

However, behind all these words is a life that is lived in joy, happiness, and creativity. *Say Yes to Your Spirit* is about enjoying the world in which we live, celebrating the relationships we are fortunate to have, and being in daily gratitude for the prosperity we will create. When we are dancing in God we have a smile on our faces. We have energy to take the necessary steps, and our style is divine.

Today I am enthusiastic
about my life.

Humility

To lead people, walk behind them.
—Lao-tzu

Say Yes to Your Spirit is about nurturing ourselves and other people. I have always felt nurtured by people who gently suggest what I might do, consider, or change, rather than those who dictate.

This is what I believe Lao-tzu is talking about: how we can lead people with gentleness.

In this book we have discussed how religion has often dictated to people, judged certain people, and instilled fear, with the result being that many people have given up and left the church. Spirituality is less severe. It accepts that there are many paths to God, and healthy spiritual leaders are gentle, not dogmatic.

When I was a young priest I felt it was my duty to be out in front leading my congregation. Today I am comfortable sitting in the back pew.

Humility comes from knowing that we are all equally important in the eyes of God.

Resentments

Anger will never disappear so long as thoughts of resentment are cherished in the mind. Anger will disappear just as soon as thoughts of resentment are forgotten.

—Gautama Buddha

How do I deal with resentments? Actually I don't have many, if any, resentments today. But I have had them. What I find helpful is the physical act of writing them down on paper. Then I can see them.

I read them to myself and ask what these resentments are really about? Did the person intend to hurt me? Am I being overly sensitive? Have I misunderstood what was said or done? At some point I always talk to the person concerned. I feel better telling them what I think or how I am feeling.

Then I try to let it go. Occasionally I will take the writing and burn it . . . a funeral pyre. It has worked for me. Today I have no resentments.

I do not allow my resentments to fester.

Personality

By nature, men are nearly all alike; by practice, they get to be wide apart.
—Confucius

In the 12-step program it says that we should put "principles before personalities." True, but it doesn't say "principles instead of personalities"!

I know that I am a personality. I can be decidedly eccentric. Although I'm a Christian, I don't believe all that the church teaches. I'm in recovery, but I don't agree with everything 12-step people say. I know I am an individual.

Of course I also know that I am human. I share certain emotions with all human beings: fear, anger, love, guilt, shame, joy, and helplessness. I belong, and yet in some ways I am apart.

Say Yes to Your Spirit is a celebration of difference with the *oneness* of being human. Each person's dance is necessarily unique, and this is a good thing.

Today I am able to celebrate my uniqueness within the human family.

Energy

To the mind that is still, the whole universe surrenders.

—Lao-tzu

There is definitely a mystical aspect in *Say Yes to Your Spirit.*

As a religious man I rarely thought about the universe. I was consumed by dogma, Scripture, and ritual. However, as I began to understand more about spirituality and its distinction from religion, I became aware of the universe. Imagine that!

Today I am concerned about the universe, especially the responsibilities I have to the Earth. There is an energy in the universe that proclaims the creativity of God, and this energy connects with my life. If I keep this connection healthy, then I am able to be successful and productive: cocreation.

Dancing in God is the act of connecting with the energy that emanates in the universe and that makes me powerful as a human being.

I celebrate the energy that connects me to the universe.

Service

Thousands of candles can be lighted from a single candle, and the life of the candle will not be shortened. Happiness never ceases by being shared.

—Gautama Buddha

I know I have influenced thousands of people over the years. Just as many people sharing have influenced me.

A Holocaust survivor told me that Jews write about, talk about, share stories about, even create films about the horrors because if they don't, they feel that it could return. The Jews are a people of remembrance.

Recovery and healing are much the same. We share about the pain and abuse, write about it, share stories about it, and occasionally create films depicting it so that we can let go and others can heal. We are candles that choose to share our flame.

When we make the decision to do this, we *Say Yes to Your Spirit.*

I share my story so that
I might continue to heal.

Forgiveness

Things that are done, it is needless to speak about. . . . Things that are past, it is needless to blame.
—Confucius

For too many years I lived in shame: what I had done, what I had said, the people whom I had hurt, the tears that had been shed . . . all created by me.

Then a wise friend said, "Get over it."

This sentence made the difference. Sometimes there are right words that are heard at the right time. I was living in the past. What I had *done*.

I needed to forgive myself. My life today is not what it was, but I was hurting my potential by continuing to wallow in the past. *Say Yes to Your Spirit* is about being in the moment and looking forward to the future.

The idea of dancing in God is to set the tone of daily celebration, an optimism based on realized change for the better.

On a daily basis I am improving.

Only when I can forgive myself
can I truly dance.

Respect

When you are content to be simply yourself and don't compare or compete, everybody will respect you.

—Lao-tzu

In recovery I am familiar with the idea of working on my character defects—those things that stop me from being the positive and creative person I was intended to be. God made me in love to love; however, some behaviors and attitudes stopped me from being a loving person.

Was there anything in particular? Well, when I tried to be you instead of me, things became crazy. Also, when I considered difference to be a threat, I became combative because of fear.

What changed? I surrendered. When I began to accept who I am and the culture I came from, then I was able to accept and respect you.

Respect is a key ingredient in
Say Yes to Your Spirit.

Purity

If a man's mind becomes pure, his surroundings will also become pure.
—Gautama Buddha

Over the years I have tried to do a yearly spring cleaning on my mind. I take a personal inventory on how I am doing. Usually I divide it into the following:

- Relations with God
- Personal healing
- Relations with family
- Relations with friends
- Professional improvements

I have always considered this to be an essential part of my personal recovery, and it definitely has a connection with the purity of my soul: pure, meaning "clean."

I don't want negative thoughts or destructive behaviors in my life, and so I need to do this spring cleaning. It is an important part of my *Say Yes to Your Spirit*. It also allows me to dance freely in God.

I seek a spiritual clarity
in my life.

Hardship

The scholar who cherishes the love of comfort is not fit to be deemed a scholar.
—Confucius

I disagree with Confucius. I feel a certain nervousness in saying this because Confucius is renowned for his wisdom. However, what is wrong with comfort?

There has always been a branch of religion, even spirituality, that has criticized luxury and physical pleasures: a religious emphasis on poverty, chastity, and rigorous obedience. This attitude encourages us to escape the physical pleasures for an otherworldly spirituality.

For me, *Say Yes to Your Spirit* is enjoying what you enjoy. Some people enjoy going into the forests with a tent, cooking food on an open fire. I enjoy a four-star hotel with a Jacuzzi. Different strokes for different folks!

The saint can dance on the top of a rugged mountain or in a Miami ballroom. Comfort is in knowing that God is involved in everything!

I enjoy and am grateful for
all the pleasures that God
has given me.

Spirituality

Spirituality is a willingness to serve.

—Leo Booth

How many times do we hear it said, "If you want to keep something, you must be prepared to give it away"?

In the 12-step program, we are reminded that service enables us to get out of ourselves. We begin to think about others rather than stay a prisoner of self. A friend said recently, "If you feel you need a drink, get out of the house and find somebody to help. It will keep you sober."

Say Yes to Your Spirit involves service. We dance in God and in the process entertain others.

I feel good when I'm helping somebody. My life is meaningful when I can bring joy into another person's life. What I give, I receive back in abundance!

Service is the loving aspect of investment.

My Say Yes to Your Spirit
involves service.

Service

Only a life lived for others is a life worth living.
—Albert Einstein

Yesterday's meditation involved a similar theme and it was headed "spirituality." Today we are asked to think about service. Of course the two are intertwined: the spiritual life involves an appreciation of others, which must include service.

Albert Einstein provides an interesting twist. He suggests that it is in our own interest to be of service to others.

- When we love another, we get to feel love.
- When we assist another, we get to feel good about who we are.
- When we forgive somebody, we feel the relief that comes with forgiveness.

The good life is in our own interest. Spirituality, however we may understand the word, benefits our life.

In service we become worthy.

I give because I have been given.

Creativity

The superior man is modest in his speech,
but exceeds in his actions.
—Confucius

I really don't like loud people. It irritates me when somebody on a cell phone is telling the listener that they are now getting on the airplane, following a lady with a large suitcase, moving toward their seat, sitting near the window, watching the other passengers find their seat, and so on, and so on. Do I really need to hear this? Does the listener need to hear this? So many people are talking and saying nothing!

Say Yes to Your Spirit is really about respect for other people, which involves what we say, who we say it to, and the manner in which we deliver the message. I shouldn't be hearing your private conversations.

People often speak to appear important. Confucius reminds us that actions are indeed louder than words. Respect is discovered in the way we treat other people. What we create with our lives, the actions reveal *Say Yes to Your Spirit*.

Today I focus on making the
action fit the word.

Conscience

Never do anything against conscience even if the state demands it.
—Albert Einstein

For too many years I had a lazy conscience. I did not think too much about right and wrong, noble or cowardly, giving or selfish. Ethically, I was bankrupt.

Then I began to discover the essence of spirituality. It explained what I truly believed about God's presence and how it related to me. I experienced the suffering in the world, and I knew that I could make a difference. I discovered that I had a conscience.

- I couldn't lie without feeling uncomfortable.
- When I hurt somebody unjustly, I felt guilty.
- God became a living reality, not a word in a book.
- Divine freedom came at a cost.

Conscience! Spiritually, I knew that there were times when I would have to stand alone. *Say Yes to Your Spirit* helps me to be prepared.

I know that I am more
than I think I am.

Letting Go

When you have faults, do not fear to abandon them.
—Confucius

A few years ago I wrote a popular book called *The Wisdom of Letting Go*. In the book I suggested that it is easier to live a healthy life than an unhealthy life. It is easier to be positive than wallow in negativity. It is easier to tell the truth than live the life of a liar.

However, to live this life, which in this book we call *Say Yes to Your Spirit*, we all need to let go of behaviors and attitudes that are not healthy, beliefs that are toxic, relationships that are dysfunctional.

"But that is hard," I hear you say. No, it is a tougher life not to let go of negative behaviors, but we are not told this. Indeed most people hear messages that reinforce the negative: "It is hard to stop drinking/eating/judging/meeting negative people." Actually it isn't. But if we keep hearing or saying it is, then it will be. What we say, we create.

I affirm my divine power of choice.

Victory

We seek victory—not over any nation or people—but over ignorance, poverty, disease, and human degradation whenever they may be found.
—Franklin Delano Roosevelt

Spirituality always enables. It tells the person to take the high road rather than the easy path. It reminds people that they carry divinity within them, and at times they will be called upon to express this miracle.

In human history, there have always been men and women who have demanded that we demonstrate the best that we can be. Some of these people, like Franklin D. Roosevelt, are world renowned. Others are ordinary people living extraordinary lives.

- They fight for justice daily in the courts.
- They defend the homeless and oppressed.
- They risk their lives as police officers or firefighters.
- They work with the mentally challenged.
- They offer their services to third world countries.

Say Yes to Your Spirit is often about the little David fighting the mighty Goliaths and winning.

No wonder we dance in God!

I can make the world a better place.

Golden Rule

What you do not want done to yourself,
do not do to others.
—Confucius

For many years I have said that religion often keeps people apart, but spirituality teaches the whole world to hold hands. Often religion can separate; spirituality is like a golden thread that connects us all together.

Jesus said to love God and your neighbor as yourself.

Wise philosophers have suggested that we treat people the way we would like to be treated.

Now, in the teaching of Confucius we read the same concept reversed: "What you do not want done to yourself, do not do to others."

Some things are just true. It doesn't really matter who says it or what words are used. The sentiment makes sense.

Say Yes to Your Spirit makes sense. Dancing in God makes sense. Being positive and creative makes far more sense than the opposite.

God is love, that's God's business!

When I know what I need to be happy,
I understand the world's needs.

December

Eternity

A good man never dies.

—Callimachus

When we begin to explain *Say Yes to Your Spirit* we realize that life is more than flesh and bones; it contains something that many have called the soul.

But what is the soul? I believe it is connected to the Mind of God, *something* that is divine and therefore does not die when we die.

I've met people who have told me that they had a previous existence, years ago, and they were an Egyptian slave or an African warrior. I've never had such an experience. Others have shared with me that they had a near-death moment and were surrounded by a white light. Again, I've not had such an experience.

But I do believe that the energy of who we are continues after death. I feel the presence of my mother and father, who died some years ago. Their wisdom is still directing me. In this sense I've experienced eternity.

The essence of who I am
continues after death.

Judgment

Don't wait for the last judgment—it takes place every day.

—Albert Camus

As a child I was scared to hear the stories of the Last Judgment. I had this image of me standing before the throne of God, quaking in my shoes, watching a bearded God scroll down a list of my sins. In my imagining I sensed that I would be sent to hell.

Today, with the philosophy of *Say Yes to Your Spirit*, I believe God is a loving presence that is alive in me. Judgment, a word I rarely use, involves discernment and understanding. If I must answer for my life, it is in the knowledge that I'm surrounded by love. The pressure is off!

I know I am my harshest critic. I believe that people judge more severely than God. As I dance in God I'm trying to remember that all is well and I have nothing to fear in God's presence.

I celebrate God's loving presence in my life.

Love

Love your neighbor as yourself.

—Jesus

This is my Golden Rule. My love of God is expressed in how I treat my neighbor and myself. Why? Because God is my neighbor—and God is also in me.

Throughout this book I've suggested that words paint a picture and we should allow our imaginations to soar; our neighbor is also this planet and the universe. How can we love if we abuse the home that is feeding us? How can we respect ourselves or our neighbor if we do not stand in wonder at the universe?

Say Yes to Your Spirit always encourages us to embrace the big picture. A connection in life unites everything.

I used to think small: *my* God, *my* church, *my* religion, *my* world. *Say Yes to Your Spirit* has changed me; the universe is being experienced in my everyday life.

Love is a cosmic force.

I'm aware today that I'm dancing with and in the universe.

Challenges

If there is no struggle there is no progress.
—Frederick Douglass

I've heard the theory so many times, and yet it still feeds my imagination: the pearl in the oyster originates with a speck of grit. Irritation creates perfection.

And this theory has a reality in my life:

- I'm a better person because of my struggles with alcoholism.
- The pain has helped to create my gains in life.
- My failings have helped me understand the failings in others.
- The experiences of my dark side have given depth to my insights concerning spirituality.
- Gut-wrenching therapy has given me an insight into my family and myself.
- My struggle has created my pearl.

When I look around at the society in which I live, I see that Frederick Douglass was correct: progress comes in proportion to the struggle.

My dance in God has not come easily.

Ancestry

Every man is a quotation from all his ancestors.
—Ralph Waldo Emerson

What a wonderful statement. What I most enjoy about this thought by Ralph Waldo Emerson is that it connects me to my ancestors.

In my culture, unlike the Native American or Chinese culture, we rarely think or speak about our ancestors. Apart from a few uncles and aunts, I know very little about my family. I never thought of past family members having an influence on my life today.

However, since exploring the concepts of *Say Yes to Your Spirit* I'm beginning to think in terms of life being a continuum. I'm connected to my people who went before. How? Genetically, emotionally, and mentally. I can understand today that I am the mixed result of my ancestors.

However, I'm not them. I'm still unique. But it feels good to acknowledge them in my life.

I'm unique but not brand new!

Religion

Men make the gods, women worship them.

—Sir James Frazer

This statement seems decidedly sexist. However, not so many years ago it was probably true.

I heard somebody once say that religion is man-made; spirituality is God-given. With a few exceptions, men have dominated religion, and they created a male God in their image.

Say Yes to Your Spirit encourages the feminine energy in our understanding of God. When I was an Episcopal priest I initially was against women in the priesthood; I understand today that my views were based on prejudice, which in turn was based on ignorance. Today I welcome women into ministry, and I've had wonderful experiences with the women ministers and priests with whom I have been fortunate enough to work. I also believe today that both the feminine and masculine energy is at work in *Say Yes to Your Spirit*.

Healthy religion, which must include the dynamic of change, is alive and evolving. And a healthy religion has women included in its leadership.

I affirm the feminine energy that is within me.

Time

Time is money.

—Benjamin Franklin

When I was drinking I wasted time. Indeed I wasted everything when I was an alcoholic.

Today I respect time. Time is part of my *Say Yes to Your Spirit*. It is what makes up my day. Time is my life.

Time needs to be managed, however, or it can so easily get away from us. Then we discover we have wasted the day. Here are some of the things I seek to do to manage my use of time:

- Write down the evening before what I want to achieve for the next day.
- Balance work and play in each day.
- Remember that less is more; if I can do three things each day, then I achieve more than exhausting myself in any given day.
- Remember to walk after lunch.
- Start the day with a prayer; end the day with a gratitude thought.

My stewardship of time
has contributed to my prosperity.

God

I turned to speak to God about the world's despair; But to make bad matters worse, God wasn't there.

—Robert Frost

I've often felt that I turned to God and nobody was there. I've felt that my prayers weren't answered. Bishop John Robinson called it "experiencing the divine absence."

Today I find God all around me: I hear God in the birds, feel God in the wind, experience God in my personal feelings.

What changed? I changed. I viewed God as a large human being that existed beyond the clouds. Because of this mind-set I limited my relationship with God to that of any other human being. God was really Mr. God!

Say Yes to Your Spirit has changed my thinking. I now believe that I am intimately involved in God; I have a divine nature. The more I'm involved in my life and creation, the more I hear God . . . but it is not a voice.

I hear and feel the Presence.

Usually, when I can't find God
it is because I'm lost.

Prosperity

Poverty borders on denial of God.

—Saadi

If I am in God and God is unlimited . . . then I am unlimited.

If I am in partnership with God and God is abundance . . . then I share in that abundance.

If I reflect God and God is perfect love . . . then I am living in a state of love.

If I am touched by God the Healer and have been given the power to heal . . . then health is my choice.

If the God of prosperity has shared his cloak with me . . . then I am wrapped in riches.

If I am anchored in a God of hope . . . then I should never fear the future.

If I am breathing the energy of God . . . then my life is amazingly creative.

It really is about what I believe. All the above is discovered in *Say Yes to Your Spirit*.

My dance in God is appropriate.

Fanaticism

Fanaticism consists in redoubling your effort when you have forgotten your aim.
—George Santayana

My work involves counseling people who have addiction issues. A patient asked me recently: "How can you be a religious addict? Surely to spend every moment of your life consumed by God would be heaven. Can you pray too much? Worship too much? According to you, Leo, the saints were religious addicts."

I think some of the saints were religious addicts.

I think you can do anything to extreme and it becomes dangerous; think about how some people have abused food and sex.

If your baby is hungry and crying, stop praying, get off your knees, and get some food.

If you are unemployed, don't spend your time worshiping. Get a job.

Religious addiction is an aspect of fanaticism. It abuses God and religion to experience a spiritual high. Like every other addiction it abuses the sufferer and will eventually destroy family and friends.

My relationship with God is balanced.

Ignorance

Our lives are universally shortened by ignorance.
—Herbert Spencer

Abuse and prejudice, which are the twin enemies of *Say Yes to Your Spirit*, are usually based upon ignorant statements that are never questioned.

- The Jews control the financial institutions and in this way control the world.
- The countries that are governed by black people are invariably third world countries, revealing that black people are inferior to white people.
- If one alcoholic drink is good, then two is better!
- God has said that woman was created to comfort man; if you disagree, then you are arguing with God.
- God told people that if they continued to sin, God would punish them. Now we see gay people dying of AIDS. They were warned!

Millions have died or are suffering because of ignorant statements, like those above, that few questioned.

My God wants me to use my brain.

Hope

It is hope that maintains most of mankind.

—Sophocles

Say Yes to Your Spirit is really about hope. It is a hope based upon the belief that life is good, created by a God who wants only the best for us . . . but we must want the same—not only want the same, but be prepared to do the things that make our life enjoyable and meaningful.

Why do some people not have this hope? Many reasons: abuse, addiction, poverty, negative messages, a belief in a vindictive and judgmental God. The list could go on and on.

If we do not heal this abusive baggage, then hope withers and dies. We cannot dance in God if we believe that God is not on our side.

Say Yes to Your Spirit is a philosophy that is really grounded in positive thinking. If we think positive thoughts, then we will live a positive and creative life.

Jesus said, "I came that you might have life and have it abundantly."

I know that life is good,
and this I affirm.

Sanity

Sanity is a cozy lie.

—Susan Sontag

I don't agree with Susan Sontag. It is a clever statement, but it is decidedly cynical.

I believe that sanity is a product of *Say Yes to Your Spirit*. It is seeing the world the way it really is rather than living in a world of fantasy.

When I was drinking I lived in a world that was anchored in what I wanted it to be rather then how it truly is; it was magical thinking. I refused to accept the obvious, that drinking was making me sad, tired, angry, confused, and lonely. However, because I didn't want to accept this, didn't want to accept that alcohol was making my life chaotic, I lived a life of denial. Now that is insanity.

In recovery I found sanity. I found a cozy life, a life that is good.

That is why I am dancing in God.

I embrace sanity, and that brings reality on a daily basis.

Calm(ness)

Make haste slowly.

—Suetonius

When I was leading a group of Americans in China, the translator came to me and said, "Don't be in such a hurry. Tell the group to take it easy. Rushing around is not a good way to experience China. Slowly is good."

I've never forgotten that intervention: slowly is good! When we embrace *Say Yes to Your Spirit* we seek to live smarter, not harder.

W. H. Davies said it so well:

What is this life if, full of care,
We have no time to stand and stare?

An aspect of living the spiritual life is to enjoy the moment. Find God in the small things; indeed, find God in the life that is all around us.

Hear the birds sing. Enjoy the leaves that hang from the trees. Smile at the faces that pass you by. Feel the rain.

Haste is a waste!

I am dancing in God . . . slowly.

Diversity

So many men, so many opinions.

—Terence

Say Yes to Your Spirit would agree with Terence, with one important exception. *Say Yes to Your Spirit* would seek to include women.

For too many years women have been excluded from philosophical statements; indeed, theology for years excluded the feminine not only in its philosophy but also in the people who were allowed to do the thinking.

- God was male.
- Males control most religions.
- Women were seen as inferior.
- Women were occasionally blamed for sin coming into the world.

This type of thinking has created so much overt and covert abuse in the world; women have suffered . . . and so have men. You cannot ignore half the population without the other half being abused as well.

Say Yes to Your Spirit tells us that there are many paths to God, and *everyone* has a right to discover the path and dance along.

It is our respectful disagreements
that make life interesting.

Freedom

I disapprove of what you say, but I will defend to the death your right to say it.
—S. G. Tallentyre (Evelyn Beatrice Hall)

Freedom involves an acceptance of diversity. We are not the same; we don't think the same, look the same, act the same, or need the same. We are all individuals. *Say Yes to Your Spirit* embraces this awareness and seeks to enjoy it.

Dictatorship, dogma, and control seek to hinder and curtail this freedom, believing that there is a right way for everyone. I don't think so.

God has created this world to include delightful differences, and often I find people saying things that I disagree with, doing things that do not appeal to me, believing things that make little sense to me. That's life. And I prefer the life that God has created to a life of controlled uniformity.

Oh yes, and over the years I've changed my mind. And that is perfectly okay in our dance in God.

Our respectful disagreements make life interesting.

Moderation

The golden rule is moderation in all things.
—Terence

I didn't know that Terence had talked with my mother!

When I was young I would hear, on a regular basis, the kitchen philosophy that happened in our house:

- Moderation in all things.
- Treat people the way you would like to be treated.
- Don't judge in ignorance.
- Think before you speak.
- Too many cooks spoil the broth.
- Silence is golden.

I'm sure you heard similar statements; they were useful and made me think. *Say Yes to Your Spirit* is respectful of moderation because it fears extremism. As St. Paul wrote, "We know only a little, but then face to face."

Addiction, obsession, compulsion, and fanaticism are all scary because they eventually suffocate gentle moderation. They kill flexibility. I need to be free to dance in God.

I seek to embrace on a daily basis
the gift of moderation.

Money

There can be no liberty unless there is economic liberty.
—Margaret Thatcher

Money is not evil. It is not something to be avoided. It need not conflict with living *Say Yes to Your Spirit*.

Years ago my mother said that anybody who tells you that money isn't important, has it!

And she was right. If you can't afford to feed your child, live in a safe neighborhood, or occasionally treat yourself to a relaxing vacation . . . then, believe me, money is important.

Notice that I said "important." But it is not the only thing in life that is important. And it is not the *most* important thing in our life. However, it is important.

When we *Say Yes to Your Spirit* we seek to embrace a life of joy and personal satisfaction that enables us to find God in everything. But more than this, it places us within the divine energy.

And money can really help us create wonderful things in the world.

Money is, for many people,
the route to freedom.

Nationalism

Rule Britannia! Britannia rules the waves;
Britons never shall be slaves.
—James Thomson

Nationalism is not a bad thing. However, like almost everything in life it can become abusive and divisive.

To be proud of your country, heritage, or culture is a step to self-esteem, but if it is used to put others down or make them feel inferior, then we have corrupted a gift.

Say Yes to Your Spirit seeks to affirm who we are and at the same time rejoices in the diversity of creation. This is also true with regard to religion; it is great to enjoy being of a certain faith, but we can also celebrate those who have a different faith. Indeed, we not only celebrate diversity in religion; we need it. It helps us to think, grow, and consider different points of view. Also, we can appreciate those who have no religion or why they do not believe.

I not only dance in God; I also dance in diversity.

Today I understand that I am a citizen of the world.

Love

I believe that love produces a certain flowering of the whole personality which nothing else can achieve.

—Ivan Sergeevich

I suppose the word "love" is the most admired word in the spiritual language. It says so much, means so much, and it is a quality that everyone wants.

Say Yes to Your Spirit affirms that love is our foundation. Love is who we are. And love connects us with other people and the universe.

I've said before in this book that we all need, at times, to be poetic: love is the language of poetry. Love encourages us to use our imagination and seek to discover and describe God in new and exciting ways. Love encompasses other words: passion, beauty, forgiveness, healing, . . . and dance.

When I dance in God I'm expressing my love for the universe. It is my *Say Yes to Your Spirit.*

I love to love.

Confidence

We are not interested in the possibilities of defeat.
—Queen Victoria

In recent years I've come to the conclusion that a practical definition of "spirituality" is being a positive and creative person.

To be confident about your life, it is essential that you believe that God is on your side and created you with unlimited possibilities. You will not find an emphasis on original sin in *Say Yes to Your Spirit*.

When we say that we are dancing in God, it conjures up the vision of confidence as well as happiness.

Research shows that people who awake believing that it is a good day are likely to achieve more than those who believe everything around them is doom and gloom.

Queen Victoria had a long and successful reign because she believed that it was her inheritance.

I am a child of a powerful God, and that makes me powerful.

I awake believing that
I will be successful.

Apathy

Apathy is a vice.
—Oscar Wilde

Say *Yes to Your Spirit* affirms that, if we choose, we can have a positive influence on our lives and the lives of others. Spirituality is a gift that we do not have to earn, but we need to use.

The apathetic people whom I've met exude a negative energy. Although they may not overtly speak defeat, they have a demeanor and energy that seems to be saying, "This is not going to work."

Have you ever tried to dance with somebody who won't even try? A reluctant partner is really no partner at all!

To dance in God and celebrate *Say Yes to Your Spirit*, it is essential to believe that God is working through us and that we all can create a loving and harmonious world.

In partnership with God and each other, we can create a world that is respectful and peaceful.

Creativity is my true nature.

Security

Security is a kind of death.
—Tennessee Williams

I appreciate the sayings that begin each daily meditation in this book because they make us think. Tennessee Williams is suggesting that security is to be avoided. Wow. Most of us have spent our lives figuring out ways to be secure . . . financially, emotionally, and socially.

Yet I understand what he is saying; if we are to think and move out of the safety zone that can easily suffocate us, we need to risk. *Say Yes to Your Spirit* is not really associated with playing it safe.

Should I be radical? A revolutionary? Maybe. Jesus challenged people to reexamine their religious teachings. Gandhi suggested that peaceful protest was a tool to healing oppression. Mother Teresa affirmed that every child is our responsibility.

When we make the decision to dance in God, we must realize that the steps change frequently!

My Say Yes to Your Spirit *involves risk—*
a willingness to think out of the box.

Incarnation

And the word became flesh.

—John 1:14

I love the Christian teaching that is often called the incarnation; God became what we are so that we might become what God is.

Jesus is seen by many as the only true Son of God. We place him on a divine pedestal and worship the life he lived. For nearly two thousand years Jesus has been seen as perfect, and everyone else sinful.

Say Yes to Your Spirit is gently suggesting that we reconsider this teaching and consider that we are all sons and daughters of God; more than this, we are divine reflections of creative divinity. There is a universal incarnation that suggests that wherever we are, God truly is. Blasphemy! For some yes, but Jesus seemed to suggest this concept when he told his disciples, "Greater things than I have done, you will do."

Dancing in God breaks down the barrier between being human and being divine.

Today I understand that divinity
is my essential nature.

Miracle

Rudolf the red-nosed reindeer had a very shiny nose.

—Robert L. May and Johnny Marks

My work involves helping those who often feel depressed, lonely, abused, . . . in a word, different. Addicts often say that they always wanted to feel on the inside what they saw other people appearing on the outside.

Rudolf's red nose made him appear different, and with this difference came the shame. Anyone who has experienced racism, sexism, homophobia, poverty, or physical disfigurement knows how Rudolf felt. Then he was called to *use* his difference, to use the years of shame to create a uniqueness that was essentially divine. Santa asked Rudolf to *Say Yes to Your Spirit.*

Miracle comes in knowing that we are essentially divine. Our inherited sinfulness is an illusion.

As I said in my book *When God Becomes a Drug*, unhealthy religion tells you what you are not, while spirituality tells you who you are.

My red nose is the key to success.

Youth

It takes a very long time to become young.
—Pablo Picasso

I had a mother who, even in her eighties, was young at heart. In the nursing home, before her death at ninety-one, she had a picture of Leonardo DiCaprio hanging on her wall!

When Pablo Picasso is talking about being young, he is not talking about age but rather the way people view themselves and the world. Are you still excited about life?

Some people seem to be born with a negative approach to life; life is out to get them! Then there are those who live *Say Yes to Your Spirit*. Regardless of age they are still excited about life and the possibilities that life affords. They are the optimists, the people who live each affirmation. Even when life throws them a hurtful curve, they look for that silver lining.

They may not know it, but they are dancing in God.

I seek excitement in every aspect of my life.

Divinity

It is a man's goal to grow into the exact likeness of God.
—Plato

I was raised with the idea that I was born in sin. I was told that human beings are essentially evil and that only through the shedding of Jesus's blood could we be saved. I was told in clear and certain terms that if you did not repent, accept Jesus, and live a Christian life, then you would go to hell.

As a young man, I had a fear of God and a fear of life.

But I never truly believed what I was told. I sensed as a young man that God not only loved me but was involved in my life. I sensed that other religions and cultures reflected God in this world, and spiritually that we were all saying similar things . . . except for the fanatics!

I still believe this. My *Say Yes to Your Spirit* affirms that I am essentially a divine creature living in a human body . . . and God wants me to play.

Where is God?
Within me and around me!

Poetry

When power corrupts, poetry cleanses.

—John F. Kennedy

Throughout this book I've suggested that poetry is a language that best seeks to explain the mystery and universality of *Say Yes to Your Spirit*.

How do you really explain God or our relationship and involvement with the Divine? Can we really explain in prose how we feel? Most people cannot.

Poetry, however, allows us to live within a concept, and although it cannot explain our daily dance in God, it paints a picture that feeds the imagination.

Poetry heals. Poetry cleanses. Poetry brings hope with words, not unlike the power of music.

Mysticism lives strongly within spirituality . . . and when we think we understand, then it surprises.

The poet within me knows that
I will never really know.

Soul

Only a free soul never grows old.

—Jean Paul Richter

As the years go by I feel younger. Why? Because I'm learning to let go of many things and discover what is real in my life.

Say Yes to Your Spirit is about being free: free to think, free to explore new ideas, free to move beyond the narrow confines of religion and explore the universal challenge that spirituality affords. This journey energizes me, and in this sense I feel younger.

I also realize today that I have a divine power that exists within me and is in creation, taking me beyond death.

What does the afterlife look like? Is it anything like I was told as a child when I heard messages about heaven? I don't know. And I don't really care.

My dance in God feels endless, and that's enough for me.

I seek the freedom that
feeds my soul.

Art

To the artist there is never anything ugly in nature.

—August Rodin

I am so pleased that I appreciate art. I have some friends who tell me they hate art, or don't understand it, or worse, feel it is unnecessary.

That has never been my experience. At school I discovered that art spoke to me in a way that science and mathematics never could. I understood that poetry was challenging me to think beyond the mere definition of words. Music spoke about a world that was not separated by geography. Before I knew what I was doing, I was dancing in God.

This is what *Say Yes to Your Spirit* means to me. It requires that I think outside the box and enter the miraculous world of mystery: God's world. And now it is my world.

I don't see ugliness anymore,
I only see difference.